Third Edition

HUMAN BEHAVIOR

A Perspective for the Helping Professions

Robert L. Berger
Thomas More College

Ronald C. Federico
Iona College

James T. McBreen
Family Outreach Services of Beech Acres

Longman
New York & London

Human Behavior: A Perspective for the Helping Professions, Third Edition

Longman, 95 Church Street, White Plains, N.Y. 10601

Associated companies:
Longman Group Ltd., London
Longman Cheshire Pty., Melbourne
Longman Paul Pty., Auckland
Copp Clark Pitman, Toronto

Senior editor: David J. Estrin
Production editor: Janice Baillie
Cover design: Tony Alberts
Text art: Fine Line Inc.
Production supervisor: Kathleen M. Ryan

Library of Congress Cataloging in Publication Data

Berger, Robert
    Human behavior : a perspective for the helping professions /
  Robert L. Berger, Ronald C. Federico, James T. McBreen.—3rd ed.
      p. cm.
    Includes bibliographical references and index.
    ISBN 0-8013-0414-8 (pbk.)
    1. Social case work.   2. Human behavior.   I. Federico, Ronald C.
  II. McBreen, James T.   III. Title
  HV43.B45   1991
  361.3′2—dc20   90-38326
                                                         CIP

1 2 3 4 5 6 7 8 9 10-MU-9594939291

Contents

Preface

INTRODUCTION

April Savino robbed her grandmother and attacked her mother with a carving knife. She also cared for infirm homeless women, making sure they were fed and clothed. Ultimately, April ended her life by shooting herself through the head on the steps of a church (Hevesi, 1988).

While it is not uncommon to read about troubled individuals like April in the newspaper, most of us wonder why people do such things. What makes a person exploit relatives and physically attack parents? How is it possible to be loving and caring toward strangers while at the same time violent with family members? And with all the social agencies that exist, why would someone feel so alone and hopeless that suicide seems the best solution?

Becoming an effective helping person involves understanding human behavior in its many forms. The horrifying and the heartwarming, the commonplace and the unique, all are part of the human situations in which people need help. Obviously many of these situations are complex, made up of elements involving individuals, families, and a wide range of life experiences in a variety of social systems. Understanding them is a difficult task that requires much knowledge and considerable sensitivity.

The goal of this book is to help you understand situations in which helping occurs. This task begins with your caring about others and your motivation to improve the quality of life for everyone. Underlying your impetus to help are knowledge, facts, and concepts about people and the systems in which they live. It is the application of your knowledge to specific people in need that will provide the base for your helping efforts. This book will focus on reviewing needed knowledge and provide you with techniques that you can use to integrate and apply that knowledge in practice. You will also learn how effective professional helpers utilize their knowledge within the context of human values and ethics.

UNDERSTANDING DREAMS

This book is about what is important to people and how these things shape their lives. People in the helping professions are in the business of enabling others to attain their life goals. To do so effectively, we must first understand what is of value to people. This is because values and goals are closely related. Humans seek what they value, and they act in ways that are consistent with their values. Therefore, professional helpers must also understand what people consider appropriate strategies to attain their goals.

Many factors influence what individuals view as important and attainable. Some of them are concrete, as when people who lack formal education find themselves excluded from desirable jobs and reluctantly give up their dream of work that is interesting and rewarding. Other factors are more intangible but nevertheless important. Religious beliefs may support a dream that says people can get along without racial conflict even though such conflict presently occurs. This book will help you understand why people have their dreams, how their behavior is affected by them, and how these dreams get modified and sometimes destroyed. As you will see when you read the case of April Savino at the end of the next chapter, she had dreams based on her own values, needs, and life experiences. Her behavior can be unraveled once we achieve some understanding of her dreams and the factors that blocked her efforts to realize them.

Understanding requires knowledge. Because the factors that influence people's dreams and values are of many kinds, the knowledge needed is diversified and extensive. This book will help you review the knowledge that you already have and, when necessary, to acquire useful new knowledge. In addition, you will learn how to use your knowledge as a professional helping person whose goal is to influence the human condition.

CLARIFYING AND ARTICULATING GOALS

In many cases the first task of the helping professional is to assist people to articulate their values and goals. Although deeply held, these values may rarely be made explicit in thought or speech. When people are helped to examine and to express their values and goals it is easier for them to consider modifying them, or to adopt alternative strategies for attaining them. Of course, individuals sometimes want things that are impossible for them to have. In these cases, acknowledging this reality with sensitivity and interpersonal support is part of what the helping professional brings to the helping process.

The values and goals that motivate human behavior are varied and often contradictory. Parents may envision their children becoming economically successful yet also want them to be caring, honest people who are ethical and not too aggressive. Other parents may have the same dream, but discourage their children from pursuing such a goal because they don't believe that it is realistic. We all have hopes and related goals for ourselves and for others, but it is sometimes difficult to establish workable priorities among them, and to sort out those that are likely to be attainable from those that are not. Professional helpers assist people as they express, clarify, and organize their dreams and goals.

TYPES OF KNOWLEDGE

A retired social worker once said that the older she became and the more practice experience she had, the less she knew. This seeming paradox is not unique to social work. Human behavior is made up of many factors operating in interaction. The result is a rich but complex network of relationships. Involved in this network are individuals; groups of people such as friends and family members; organizations like social agencies and businesses; communities; and the larger structures that constitute society as a whole. What the retired social worker was trying to say was that the more experience she had, the more she realized how complex human behavior is in its social environment. It wasn't that she knew less and less. Rather, the more she knew the more she realized there was even more to know.

There are many kinds of knowledge and it is constantly developing. The sciences, the arts, and the humanities all attempt to explain and portray the mind, body, and nature of the human person. Each type of knowledge approaches this task differently. The sciences seek consistent, predictable, and quantifiable laws that will explain human behavior (Leshan and Margenau, 1982). The arts look to the human imagination to find a vision of the essentials of human existence, while the humanities examine cultural and historical traditions to find meaning in human life. Each of these approaches creates useful knowledge.

By understanding that there are many sources of knowledge, we can avoid unidimensional views of behavior. Fritz Perls, the Gestalt psychologist, presents a useful metaphor to keep in mind as we embark on the study of human behavior. Borrowing from the language of art, he refers to the figure-ground dichotomy as we seek to understand behavior. If we attend to the apple (figure) on the table (ground), the table fades from attention. As we gaze into the night sky (ground) and imagine its immensity, we lose perspective of our place in it (figure). So also with our attempt to grasp the essence of human behavior. Each of the sciences, arts, and humanities has added something to our explanation of human behavior.

Yet by focusing on only parts of this total storehouse of knowledge we tend to emphasize the figure (specific behavior of interest to us) and lose sight of the ground (the context within which the behavior occurs).

Human behavior is more than the sum of its parts. Despite all of our scientific knowledge, there is a sense of mystery in human behavior. The most sophisticated computers were unable to predict the stock market crash of 1987, despite billions of megabytes of data. How much more complex and multitudinous the variables involved in the actions of one person in time and place.

How then can we approach the study of human behavior? The answer is—with caution. Like the physical universe, the human person is governed by the ordered and by the random. From the physical sciences we strive for predictability; from the social sciences we appreciate diversity; from the arts and the humanities we understand uniqueness and perspective. As helping professionals we must seek to learn all that is knowable while always being mindful of the incompleteness of the task. Science and mystery are not incompatible principles. They yield both knowledge and reverence.

This text develops a framework for approaching the study of human behavior that builds on an understanding of the sciences, the arts, and the humanities, and one that is useful for practice. Discerning what knowledge is important for intervention is, to use Fritz Perls' analogy, a task of separating figure from ground. The framework is also firmly rooted in social work values and practice principles. It is built on a health model of human behavior in which the human person is seen as striving for wellness and in the process of becoming.

Lest you become discouraged by the magnitude of the task, keep in mind that you already know a great deal about human behavior. In the courses you have taken in anthropology, psychology, sociology, political science, economics, and biology you have learned much about various facets of people and their behavior. The arts and humanities have furthered your awareness of the dimensions of human behavior. Building on this, the focus in this book will be on helping you review what you know, learn some techniques for integrating that broad range of knowledge, and then develop skill in applying it to real-life situations that helping people commonly encounter. The end result of your using this text, then, should be very practical. You should be more confident about what you know, and you should be able to use your knowledge to help yourself and others.

SUMMARY AND OBJECTIVES OF THIS BOOK

Let us summarize before you move on to Chapter 1. This book is intended to assist people in the helping professions to utilize knowledge in their practice. By understanding human behavior in its social context, helping professionals can make practice decisions more effectively. Several assumptions underlie this point of view:

1. Knowledge is fundamental for professionally responsible helping efforts.
2. Some knowledge is more useful for practice than other knowledge. In particular, knowledge that establishes a systems and human-diversity context for human behavior is most useful for understanding situations in which people need or want help.
3. In order to be of practical use, knowledge (in the form of concepts and data) must be learned, integrated, and applied to actual life situations. The practitioner must also know how to determine which concepts and data are most useful in specific practice situations. In addition to summarizing selected concepts, their utility for practice will be discussed.
4. The current state of our knowledge does not allow us to understand all human behavior. Thus, we encourage the reader to maintain a sense of awe and wonderment when confronted with the complexities of human action. At the same time, this book will try to illuminate as much human behavior and the richness of its social context as our present knowledge makes possible.

The book's three principal objectives derive from the above assumptions. They are summarized as follows:

1. *To systematically review and summarize concepts and data that have particular practical relevance.* Useful concepts exist in various disciplines in the biological, social, and behavioral sciences, especially sociology, psychology, political science, economics, anthropology, and human biology. In addition to summarizing selected concepts from these disciplines, their utility for practice will be discussed.
2. *To develop a framework that can be used to integrate the concepts relevant to understanding human behavior.* While individual disciplines concentrate on the teaching of discrete concepts and theories, this book will focus on finding relationships among them. This will make it easier to perceive and understand human behavior as a totality rather than as discrete, or separate, actions.
3. *To demonstrate how integrated knowledge may be used by helping professionals.* In support of this objective, we will seek to establish a context for the analysis and decision making that are essential components of practice.

FEATURES OF THIS EDITION

The major change in this edition is an extension and expansion of materials presented in the two previous editions. Faculty and students who have used previous editions of the text have suggested a broadening in scope and content to provide more depth to the material. This third edition responds to those suggestions and draws heavily from the liberal arts tradition to provide a rich tapestry for the study of human behavior and the social environment.

This edition has a more explicit linkage with the profession of social work and the health model that it uses. Illustrative materials are presented throughout to stimulate discussion about the complex nature of human behavior and the tasks confronting professional helpers. Much of the case material at the end of each chapter is new, the goal being to have current material that also provides even more effective learning opportunities.

The study questions at the end of each chapter have been revised to provide additional challenges to the student to master, integrate, and apply the concepts presented in the chapter narrative. As in the previous edition, key terms are listed for each chapter to help the reader review the central concepts and ideas presented in the chapter.

Although specific features in this edition of the text vary, what remains the same is our belief that a holistic understanding of human behavior is critical to our efforts as practitioners to be effective problem solvers. We find this challenge both daunting and exciting, something that helps us to mobilize our energies in creative and productive ways. We hope that you will experience this same excitement and challenge, and that you will find this book a helpful companion along the path to practice competence.

ACKNOWLEDGMENTS

The authors wish to acknowledge the many persons who have contributed to this revised edition. As with previous editions many students, educators, and practitioners have offered suggestions, ideas, and comments which have added to the text's development and refinement.

The technical assistance of the Longman staff has been especially helpful. David Estrin, senior editor, and Janice Baillie, production editor, have generously provided their technical assistance throughout this revision. Thanks are also extended to Jay Wilson for the index of the book and to Fine Line Inc. for the illustrative artwork.

REFERENCES

Leshan, L. and A. Margenau (1982). *Einstein's Space and Van Gogh's Sky: Physical Reality and Beyond.* New York: Collier Books, p. 7.

Hevesi, D. (1988). Running Away. *New York Times Magazine,* October 2, pp. 31ff.

CHAPTER 1

Human Behavior and Effective Practice

A better future for the families most disconnected from the nation's prosperity would require not only . . . [social welfare programs]; equally essential are policies to promote economic growth, to create more jobs and expand job training, and to assure that people who work can earn enough to support a family.

Lisbeth Schorr

CHAPTER OVERVIEW

The fact that you are considering a career in social work or in a related human service profession undoubtedly indicates your desire to be of service to people. This chapter starts with the assumption that the foundation for professional helping indeed begins with such a desire. The chapter then focuses on why knowledge is important for effective professional helping and discusses the kind of knowledge that is most useful for the human service practitioner. A health-oriented model of social work practice is presented and the implications of such a model for the study of human behavior is discussed. Issues in selecting knowledge for practice are explored prior to examining the purposes of the generalist model of social work practice. The chapter includes a look at the importance of assessment to the generalist practitioner and some thoughts on the ethical use of knowledge. Chapter 1 therefore lays the groundwork for the remainder of the book by developing a perspective on human behavior content that is grounded in professional purpose and based on a health model of social work.

1

A WORD ABOUT BEHAVIOR

Definitions of **behavior** are as diverse as the academic disciplines that seek to explain it and the professions that attempt to influence it. If you were to ask the students taking this course to define behavior, there would undoubtedly be a wide range of responses. Some would define behavior in terms of specific acts. Behavior, according to such a definition, is simply what one does. Others may suggest a broader perspective and include cognition and emotion in addition to action.

The *Social Work Dictionary* defines behavior as

> . . . any reaction or response by an individual, including observable activity, measurable physiological changes, cognitive images, fantasies, and emotion (Barker, 1987:14)

For the purposes of this book we are adopting this perspective—not so much as a definition of behavior but as a set of parameters that frame the subject matter under analysis. Such an all-inclusive definition allows the practitioner to consider behavior not only in terms of specific acts and their consequences, but also the subjective states from which such acts spring. From an assessment point of view, the practitioner may find questions such as "Why does the person behave this or that way?" less helpful than questions as to what influences, both interior and exterior, shaped or affected a given behavior. Behavior involves the interaction of three forces: the cognitive (what one thinks), affective (what one feels), and behavioral (what one does).

At the end of this chapter is an account of the life of April Savino. Coming from a middle-class family whose parents divorce, April experiences a number of events and relationships that ultimately lead to her suicide. As we try to understand April's life, our task is to identify her needs and the ways in which those needs were or were not met by the systems in which she lived. Our goal is not to blame anyone, or to identify one "cause" of her death. Instead, as practitioners we seek to understand how different factors influence behavior so that we can modify their interaction, allowing people to grow and thrive rather than to lose control over their lives.

COMMITMENT, SKILL, AND KNOWLEDGE IN PRACTICE

A central task of professional helpers is to assist people and systems to function more effectively so that individuals can attain their goals with as few obstacles and as little pain as possible (Federico, 1990: Chapter 2). Doing this involves the use of many resources, among the most important of which is the commitment and knowledge of the professional person. Without the basic commitment to help others there is neither the drive nor the desire to struggle with the complexities of effective helping. The day-to-day effort to assist individuals who are enmeshed in difficult and often painful situations yields rewards only to those who are committed to the task (Wells, 1989).

Motivated by a solid commitment to help other people, and assuming the ability to relate effectively to others, the helping professional needs a solid body of knowledge upon which to build intervention strategies. Human behavior is rich and complex. Many factors are involved in any life situation; this is especially true in situations requiring professional help. Efforts to provide help must grow out of the ability to understand problematic situations accurately as well as the resources and obstacles imbedded in them (Berelson and Steiner, 1964; Smalley, 1967; Zimbalist, 1977). No matter how committed the helping professional may be, knowledge is needed to help others effectively.

Knowledge alone, however, is not sufficient: It must be used in a caring and ethical way on behalf of others, and it must be supported by effective helping skills. Exhibit 1 at the end of this chapter illustrates the interplay of commitment, knowledge, and skill. Inadequate knowledge, skill, and commitment on the part of many professional helping persons—along with legal barriers—prevented an understanding of April's desperate situation. Although this book will focus on knowledge as a component of effective helping, keep in mind that it is only one of four essential components of helping: (1) having a commitment to helping others; (2) showing **competency** in the use of intervention skills; (3) having and using the knowledge needed to understand all significant aspects of a practice situation; and (4) utilizing knowledge and skill in ethical ways within the value base of the helping professions.

THE SOCIAL WORK HEALTH MODEL

The profession of social work has historically focused on person–environment transactions. It differs from the other helping professions in that it promotes the interaction between individuals and their environment for the betterment of both. Therefore, the point of intervention can be with the individual, the environment, or the interaction between the two. Other helping professions are more specialized in their focus. For example, medicine is concerned with physical health, psychiatry with emotional well-being, and criminal justice with lawful behavior. Social workers would include all of these dimensions in their efforts to help people to function more effectively. For instance, April Savino's case at the end of this chapter would have required a social work holistic approach to address her need for financial assistance, emotional support, housing, drug rehabilitation, health care, and education.

Of all the helping professions, only social work would attempt to put together a package of services to address all of these needs. Naturally many of the specific resources, such as health care or drug rehabilitation, would be provided by other helping professions like medicine or psychology. Making sure that they worked together in an integrated fashion would be the task of the profession of social work.

To accomplish this, the social work profession focuses on a **holistic,** systems-oriented, and health perspective in its attempt to explain human behavior and develop intervention strategies. This is summarized in the health model (Weick, 1986), which focuses on the *interaction* between people and their environment. It contrasts with the medical model, which tends to locate problems primarily *within* the person (Kagel and Cowger, 1984). In Table 1, which compares the two, you can see that the medical model (labeled the biomedical model) seeks a specific cause for a problem that is solved by experts who focus primarily on that problem.

The health model sees people as agents of change who need resources, support, and knowledge so that they can make choices that will better enable them to function in their environment. It articulates a belief in the capacity of people to become more fully human and in the dignity that inheres in this

TABLE 1. THE MEDICAL AND HEALTH MODELS COMPARED

	Biomedical Model	Health Model
Primary emphasis	Study and treatment of disease	Study and promotion of health
Orientation toward disease	Diseases as derangement of body	Ill health as expression of imbalance among interacting environments
Orientation toward health	Health as absence of disease	Health as expression of optimal well-being
Causality	Attempt to locate specific cause in biochemical and organic functioning of body (reductionistic)	Recognition of patterns among levels of influence (holistic)
Nature of intervention	Provision of externally instigated treatments	Stimulation of internal healing capacity
Role of professional	The agent of externally produced cure	The facilitator of the healing process
Role of patient	Passive but cooperative recipient of medical intervention	Active director of the healing process
Role of society	Disease is a private business; society shoulders some of the costs in its welfare function	Health is the public's business; society is responsible for creating healthy environments

(The Philosophical Context of a Health Model of Social Work, by Ann Weick, Social Casework, November 1986: Family Service America. Reprinted by permission of publisher.)

capacity. The model emphasizes a growth orientation and assumes the human person strives for a state of wellness. It focuses less on diagnosing disease or internal conflicts and more on supporting the resources of either the person or the group, assisting in problem solving, and removing obstacles to human growth and goal attainment. Whereas the medical model has a narrow focus and sees professionals as the primary agents of change, the health model sees people themselves as able to manage their own lives. The role of the professional is to provide the resources people need, whether they be personal (such as information or counseling) or environmental (such as access to job training or housing).

How behavior is viewed determines how practice is conceptualized. A direct practice model stemming from a health orientation is, for instance, suggested by Parsons, Hernandez, and Jorgensen (1988). They propose a **habilitation** versus a *rehabilitation* framework for viewing intervention. Generalist practice, according to this model, broadens the scope of points of intervention to include not only individuals and small groups like the family and friendship groups, but also larger groups such as neighborhoods, organizations, communities, and societies. Habilitation implies promoting growth and providing means to enhance problem-solving capabilities. The authors suggest that habilitation does not deny that people suffering from problems may be functioning poorly; but the focus of intervention moves from the dysfunctional behavior to competencies people have that will eventually enable them to address problems. Table 2 summarizes the differences between habilitation and rehabilitation.

The focus of the social work approach is on **empowering** individuals and groups of people to improve their ability to attain their goals. Or, as stated in the language of the preface of this book, the focus is on helping people realize their dreams.

Some theories of human behavior are more consistent with an empowering/habilitation/health approach. For example, psychoanalytic theories that view individuals as reacting to unconscious drives that are in conflict with themselves and consequently with others are not compatible with the generalist approach. Intervention based on psychoanalytic theories is dependent upon an understanding and reconciling of these internal conflicts. The practitioner's role is to direct the person's search for conflictual drives and to help resolve them through the interpretation of the person's hopes, dreams, and thoughts.

In this approach the problem is seen as being within the person and the solution rests heavily on the skill of the practitioner. Based on a disease model, the diagnosis occurs in uncovering the conflicts within the "patient" and the cure rests on the skill, knowledge, and insight of the professional. Even neo-Freudians, such as Karen Horney, who have developed a broader view of the causes of "illness" within the individual and who suggest that in addition to internal drives the person is influenced by the interaction of the individual with significant others and by society, do not have a holistic view. They still believe that the focus of attention and intervention remains with the individual.

TABLE 2. COMPARING HABILITATION AND REHABILITATION

	Habilitation	Rehabilitation
View of client	Problems between person and environment	Problem in the person
	Victim of social problem	Devalued deviant with dysfunctional condition
	Expectation of fundamental competence and learning of coping skills	Expectation of helplessness
View of client behavior	Behavior on a normative continuum	Behavior as dichotomous; abnormal or normal
	Behavior viewed in environmental context, code of cultural conventions	Behavior attributed to need, deficiency, or pathology
	Current events cause current behavior	Past events cause current behavior
	Behavior as troubling to society	Behavior as the client's problem
Relationship between social worker and client	Coequal problem solvers, each with unique expertise	Dysfunctional client and the social worker as healer
	Treatment expertise not needed, but instead education and mobilization	Expert therapist; client a recipient of service
	Risk and responsibility expected from client	Fostering of dependency of client
	Client expected to learn new coping skills and resources	Client expected to be dysfunctional due to pathology
Intervention	Intervention independent of etiology	Cause necessary for determination of cure
	Education and acquisition of new skill	Treatment and cure implied

(R. Parsons, S. Hernandez, and J. Jorgensen, Integrated Practice: A Framework for Problem Solving. Reprinted with permission from Social Work, Vol. 33(5), p. 419, Sept./Oct. 1988. Copyright 1988, National Association of Social Workers, Inc.)

This is not to say that such person-focused theories are wrong. They may well serve those helping professions that specialize in mental or physical health, such as psychoanalysis or medicine. For social work and other human-service professions that take a holistic and health-oriented view of human behavior, however, theories that minimize environmental influences on behavior are not too useful because they restrict the person–environment perspective. Ultimately a plan for intervention might include psychoanalysis, but it would include other helping efforts as well, based on a holistic assessment of people's needs and resources.

An **ecological** approach such as the one suggested by Germain and Gitterman (1986), Hartman and Laird (1983), and Pardek (1988) is more consistent with the person-in-situation perspective of social work. Human behavior is viewed from an ecological perspective as developing from a complex interplay of biological, psychological, social, economic, political, and physical forces. Therefore, theories of human behavior must take into account these interacting influences in order to be useful for the helping professions that utilize a holistic orientation. Such theories should possess these elements:

1. A health orientation, so that the person is seen as striving for health and wholeness.
2. A growth orientation, with the person seen as positively goal-directed.
3. An ecological perspective, with the person seen as influenced by multiple and interacting factors.

ISSUES IN SELECTING KNOWLEDGE

Each person at any point in time is the result of many experiences and influences from the past and from the present. Therefore, all knowledge may be potentially useful, but since we are capable of accessing and assimilating only a fraction of all available knowledge, we need some tools to use in selecting knowledge. The authors suggest the following framework for organizing types of knowledge so that the role of each in practice can be appreciated.

Types of Knowledge

Empirical	Philosophical
Specialist	Generalist
Explanatory	Intervention
Personal	

All except the *explanatory* and *intervention* categories will be discussed in this chapter. The others will be highlighted in the next chapter.

Empirical Knowledge

Empirical knowledge is based on the scientific method of inquiry. It relies on our senses—things we can hear, taste, touch, see, and smell. Empirical knowledge is that which we can measure in some concrete way. For example, we can measure the volume of a glass of water, the number of people who answer yes to the same question, or the accuracy with which people view an object.

We tend to use empirical knowledge when we want to "prove" something. In everyday life we argue over what was in a newspaper article and resolve the dispute by getting the paper and looking at what was written. The disputed statement is either there or it is not. This is a very direct and concrete measuring of an object. The sciences adopt this same basic approach, although with considerably more sophistication. Whether we are concerned with the biological, physical, social, or behavioral sciences, all attempt to measure objects of interest so that we can actually perceive and count them. Biologists count the number of white cells in blood, physicists measure the speed of light, and sociologists determine how many people have health insurance. All are efforts to measure the behavior of the real world. Empirically measured information is usually called *data* and is considered to be *fact* when repeated measurements yield the same result. Because of its emphasis on measurable fact and proof, the empirical approach is also sometimes called *positivist*.

The sciences seek to measure reality so that they can find predictable patterns in the behavior of the physical and social worlds. It is these patterns that we use to base our decisions upon. People who have a reduced number of white blood cells may have a particular disease; this is based on voluminous research that has shown a predictable relationship between reduced white blood cells in the blood and that disease. Finding out that millions of people lack health insurance may lead to governmental action to make health insurance more readily available; again, this is based on research that demonstrates that people without health insurance get sick more frequently and miss more days from work.

Helping professionals use empirical knowledge extensively. We have clients fill out questionnaires so that we get basic information such as age, income, and educational background. We also study the professional literature to learn how others have solved problems that we may be facing. We examine research data so that we are sensitized to existing problems and needs—is the incidence of teenage pregnancy increasing or decreasing? Practitioners also count events in their own practice so that they can fill out reports for the agencies for whom they work, or collect data they can use to advocate for particular legislation. Empirical data, then, are of great importance in practice.

Philosophical Knowledge

Philosophical knowledge attempts to understand universal and individual experience through rational thought rather than through the measurement of actual behavior of people or objects. Philosophical knowledge glories in the unique ability of human beings to think in highly complex thought patterns. People can process their own images of reality, which may differ from what is actually measurable, yet these may nevertheless influence behavior.

For example, Victor Frankl in *Man's Search for Meaning* notes that the atrocities inflicted on the inmates of Nazi concentration camps were designed not only to annihilate the body but also to destroy the human spirit. Yet men and women were able to rise above their suffering to live and die with dignity even when no dignity was afforded them. Through their minds they created a spirit that did not exist in the empirical, measurable world, but which nonetheless sustained them.

Although they are quite different, an important link exists between empirical and philosophical knowledge. It is the ability of people to think logically and creatively about themselves and their environment that makes it possible to imagine previously unknown linkages between elements of the real world. Once these ideas have been generated, empirical methods can be used to determine if the relationship actually exists. The testing of new treatment possibilities for diseases results from the systematic thinking about what curative agents might have an effect. Of course there are still relationships that we can logically deduce as true but that we cannot prove empirically because of limitations in our measurement tools.

Roberta Wells Imre (1984) shows how philosophical and empirical knowledge are vital to social work practice. She points out, however, that the philosophical base for social work practice has been sorely neglected in the literature. Referring to the philosopher Martin Buber's I-Thou and I-It thinking about relationships, she says:

> Human beings of necessity move back and forth between the worlds of I-It and I-Thou. It is the uniquely human quality of I-Thou relationships, however, that can be overlooked and quite possibly jeopardized in social work practice when only that which can be perceived within a conceptual framework acceptable to a positivist science [e.g., the empirical approach] is considered to be knowledge. . . . Social workers need to awaken out of acceptance of the basically positivistic position that there can be a clear-cut separation between knower and what is known, between facts that tell how the world is and what is considered to be good and valuable. In human lives empirical evidence counts; it is not all that matters. A profession intrinsically concerned with human beings requires a philosophy of knowing capable of encompassing all that is human. The language of philosophy is needed in order to address questions about what it means to be human. (p. 44)

In this statement, Imre notes that relationships between people are of critical importance to them and to our efforts to understand people. It is not just people in relationship to the physical world or to formal structures that are important. Furthermore, many questions we can only ponder, not prove. What is the meaning of life? What should the fundamental relationship of people be to each other? What is right and wrong in daily living? Although we cannot measure and prove these dimensions of existence, they are important and must not be ignored. Philosophical knowledge enables us to think about such issues in constructive ways, and Imre appeals to us not to limit our thinking only to that which is empirically provable.

Personal Knowledge and Practice

Personal knowledge is that body of knowledge that develops from our own experience. The validity of such a personal knowledge might be suspect in that it lacks the objectivity of the scientific method. Polanyi (1958:18), however, states that personal knowledge (what he calls *tacit knowledge*) is the basis of all objective knowledge (what he calls *explicit knowledge*). He further claims personal knowledge to be superior because only it is gained through true creativity. In other words, it is similar to empirical knowledge because it depends on experience—sensory experience instead of data obtained in some other way. It is nevertheless different in that it is not always measurable. Three kinds of personal knowledge are especially important: sentient, experiential, and a priori. Let us briefly look at each.

Sentient knowledge is defined by Zuboff (1988:61) as an action-centered skill based upon the sensory information derived from physical cues. Exhibit 1 at the end of Chapter 3, taken from Zuboff's book *In the Age of the Smart Machine*, provides insight into the importance of this type of knowledge to the human person. It is knowledge held by the body, and such activities as sewing, throwing a curve ball, driving a car, typing, and mountain climbing are all possible because of sentient knowledge. In this highly technological age, more and more skills are being lost in the automated production process as well as through our use of labor-saving devices.

Child-development experts believe that the basis of all subsequent cognitive and abstract learning is sensory experience. Children know the sense of roundness long before that have the language to express it or before they are able to know abstractly that balls, wheels, balloons, and pies are all round. When sentient knowledge is reduced in a "hands off" work world, profound disorientation and alienation of people from their world may result. Sentient knowledge is vital to physical and mental functioning and growth. In Polanyi's words (1958:31), "To be aware of our body in terms of the things we know and do is to feel alive. This awareness is an essential part of our existence as sensuous active persons."

Experiential knowledge is closely akin to sentient knowledge in that it is derived from contact with the environment. It differs in that the experiences are processed through the conscious mind and need not have been actually experienced by the "knower." For example, people who have been burned by a match know that they will experience similar pain if they enter a burning building. Experiential knowledge allows a person to extrapolate information from one experience to a similar experience. It is also the basis of empathy, which will be discussed further in Chapter 5.

A priori knowledge is similar to philosophical knowledge in its attempts to understand both universal and individual experience. It differs from formal philosophical knowledge in that it exists beyond rational thought, although rational thought may be used to explain a priori knowledge. Campbell (1986:27) suggests that a priori knowledge is within us from birth, whereas Jung (1968:50) believes that in addition to personal conscious and unconscious processes there exists a *collective unconscious*. This is comprised of symbols and images rooted in the human psyche. Jung suggests that the similarities among symbols and myths found in various cultures is evidence of the presence of a collective unconscious shared by humankind. Thus, such symbols as the tree of life and serpents, or legends such as the mythic hero, death and resurrection, and feral children speak to a body of knowledge common to all people.

The knowledge contained in the symbols and myths may embody a universal understanding of the nature of relationships: person to person, person to nature, person to the supernatural. This collective knowledge seems to contain within it the "wisdom of the ages." However, it must be brought to awareness by each individual. While a priori knowledge can only be inferred by examination of universal symbols and myths, it should be acknowledged as one aspect of personal knowledge. Mythical tales and symbols constantly repeat themselves in literature and art simply because they convey not only universal but also personal meaning.

Each of the three types of personal knowledge we have been discussing is relevant to the understanding of human behavior. Each is rooted in human experience: body, mind, and soul. While the nature of such knowledge is somewhat abstract, it would be unwise of the practitioner to underestimate its power.

Specialist Knowledge

Deciding what knowledge is useful for intervention partially rests on our notion of professional purpose. We must be able to state what it is that professionals do in order to identify the knowledge that will help them do their job effectively. Understanding similarities and differences among professional helpers requires that we look at two types of professional helping: specialized helping and generalist helping. Let us begin with specialists and the knowledge that they need.

A **specialist** provides specific kinds of helping services in particular types of situations. For example, a surgeon performs surgery on people who have certain kinds of illnesses, and a police officer intervenes in situations where violations of law occur. Specialized knowledge is needed to provide specialized services. None of us would entrust our body to someone who had not had special training to perform the kind of surgery we needed.

Because the focus of intervention of specialists is fairly narrow, the knowledge they need is easier to identify. Selecting knowledge begins with a specification of the actual tasks that the practitioner will have to perform. A psychiatrist, for example, writes prescriptions, supervises students in training, and practices psychotherapy. This mandates that psychiatrists have medical training, knowledge of teaching and supervisory skills, and a command of theories of psychotherapy. They are not likely to need to know other kinds of knowledge—resources available for homeless children, how to organize a rent strike, or how to form a self-help group for parents of children with learning disabilities. Specialists, then, focus their search for knowledge in areas that are related to their practice.

GENERALISTS

Generalist practitioners address the needs of the whole person and try to find the package of resources that will address the range of needs that people have. The generalist responds to multiple levels of need. If a generalist social worker was helping someone about to have surgery, for example, the help provided might include finding a competent surgeon, obtaining the money to pay for the surgery, helping the patient's family to understand the surgery and provide emotional support for the patient, arranging for post-hospital care upon discharge, and counseling the patient about any fears related to the operation.

Because generalists utilize a wide range of systems and resources in their work, the knowledge they need is extensive. However, they may need some knowledge about a lot of things rather than in-depth knowledge about a few things. Specialists are likely to need extensive knowledge about the area of their practice whereas generalists must understand enough to help people make choices, and then monitor the quality of services they receive from the service providers they choose (many of whom are probably specialists).

Generalists, Assessment, and Knowledge

Generalists also need a wide range of knowledge because they often have the responsibility to assess what help is needed. **Assessment** is the process of gathering as much information as possible about the practice situation at hand. This is the information that will generate ideas about what the causes of the problematic situation might be, and where the remedies could be found.

Let us look at causes first. If a child is being abused by its parents, it could be because its birth was unintended and the child is resented by its parents. It could also be because the child is handicapped and the parents are ashamed of it. Alternatively, the marital relationship might be disintegrating with the result that the child is being used as a scapegoat. Each of these possibilities requires knowledge of different kinds of human dynamics—some biological, some psychological, some social-structural, and some cultural. Only by patiently gathering as much information as possible can the meaningful causes be identified.

Accuracy is critical because the intervention plan that is developed will reflect the suspected causes. If the child is resented because its birth was not planned, then counseling, foster care, or even adoption might be appropriate. If the child is handicapped, then medical intervention or some relief to the parents through the provision of home health aides is possible. A direct relationship exists between perceived causes and services selected. Knowledge of the full richness of human behavior is basic to an accurate understanding of causes.

Knowing what services to offer suggests specific practice skills that will be needed, and they too require knowledge to be used successfully. What do we know about communicating with a resentful parent, or with an abused child who may be too young or too frightened to talk? What sorts of psychological issues can be anticipated with an abused child, regardless of the reasons for the abuse? These are also assessment issues.

Assessment, then, makes clear why knowledge is so important in professional helping. It helps us to understand the nature of the situation, as well as the options available to deal with it. Assessment for generalists requires a broader range of knowledge because the problems and interventions are likely to be wide-ranging. Specialists will most likely have a narrower range of problems and intervention strategies to consider in their assessment, so the knowledge they need will probably be narrower but more in-depth.

GENERALIST SOCIAL WORK PRACTICE

The most generalist of all helping professionals is the entry-level professional social worker. The generalist nature of this person's work rests on the purposes of social work, described in the following way by Baer and Federico (1978):

> Social work is concerned and involved with the interactions between people and the institutions of society that affect the ability of people to accomplish life tasks, realize aspirations and values, and alleviate distress. These interactions between people and social institutions occur within the context of the larger societal good. Therefore, three major purposes of social work may be identified:
>
> 1. To enhance the problem-solving, coping, and developmental capabilities of people;
> 2. To promote the effective and humane operation of the systems that provide people with resources, services, and opportunities;
> 3. To link people with systems that provide them with resources, services, and opportunities. (p. 68)

This view of **generalist social work practice** grows out of a holistic perspective of human behavior—the person-in-environment idea that we have already discussed. Human life is seen as a totality in which biological, psychological, cultural, and social-structural elements are in constant interaction. It is this complex world that has to be understood by the entry-level generalist professional social worker in order to find the resources that will make possible the changes needed and desired. This view begins to define the knowledge required so that the complex web of human life is understandable, an issue addressed in further detail in the next chapter.

Figure 1 graphically summarizes the points made so far. The Developmental Assessment Wheel, developed by Vigilante and Mailick (1988), is a visual attempt to unify the biological, psychological, social-structural, and cultural factors that influence human behavior. Basic human aspirations relate to goals and dreams which we discussed in the Preface. The intervening variables are the specific characteristics and life experiences of those whom we are trying to understand and serve. Social pathologies are the societal processes that impede everyone's functioning, but they may have special significance for the client(s) with whom we are working. Finally, developmental needs alert us to the life-span issues our client(s) face. We can see, then, how the Developmental

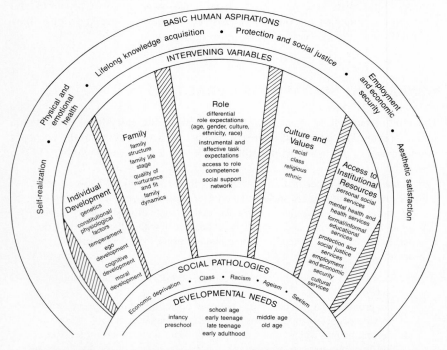

Figure 1. The Developmental Assessment Wheel (F. Vigilante and M. Mailick, Needs Resource Evaluation in the Assessment Process. Reprinted with permission from *Social Work*, Vol. 33(2), p. 103, Mar./Apr. 1988. Copyright 1988, National Association of Social Workers, Inc.)

Assessment Wheel helps the generalist social worker do a thorough evaluation. It is also clear that such a practitioner needs a wide range of knowledge in order to carry out this task.

ETHICAL CONSIDERATIONS IN THE USE OF KNOWLEDGE

Knowledge is one form of power. The knowledge we gain regarding the nature of human behavior can, if we choose, place us as professional helpers in a powerful position. People seeking help are often very vulnerable, and they place much trust in us by choosing to expose their needs to us. With our ability to assess situations we can target areas of particular vulnerability. Our knowledge of resources and intervention possibilities enables us to selectively utilize both.

A basic principle of the helping professions is that service to the client is the primary commitment of the practitioner. We must always use our knowledge in the service of others instead of for our own ease, profit, or desire to manipulate or exploit others. Even if practitioners themselves use knowledge in an ethical way, they may find themselves in work situations where there is pressure to use knowledge to manipulate others. For example, Grenier (1988) alleges that psychological knowledge was misused by Johnson & Johnson, the manufacturer of medical supplies, at one of its plants. Knowledge of group process and the desire most workers have to be accepted by their co-workers were factors used by the company to have workers pressure each other not to support a union, according to Grenier.

Practitioners have the dual responsibility to have command of the knowledge they need to practice effectively, and to use that knowledge in an ethical way to help others. Knowledge can be empirical or philosophical—both offer important insights into human behavior. The knowledge needed by generalists is likely to differ from that utilized by specialists. No matter what kind of practitioner or what kind of knowledge, the mandate is to have a solid ethical base in the use of knowledge so that our own dignity, the dignity of our profession, and that of those we serve are maintained.

SUMMARY

This chapter has emphasized the close ties between knowledge and skills that are important to people in the helping professions. No matter how much one wants to help others, the development of professional skills grows out of knowledge about the goals people have for themselves, about acceptable ways of attaining these goals, factors influencing people's behavior in problematic situations, and the helping process. The generalist approach to helping emphasizes the person-in-situation, takes a holistic view of human behavior, and adopts a health/growth/

empowerment perspective on the helping process. Effective helping occurs only when the many dimensions of problematic situations are addressed—a perspective that results from the professional having mastered a wide range of biological, behavioral, and social-science knowledge. This range of knowledge will be the focus of the next chapter.

KEY TERMS

Assessment. The process of gathering as much information as possible about the practice situation at hand.

Behavior. Any action or response including observable activity; measurable, physiological changes; cognitive images; fantasies, and emotions.

Competency. The ability to perform a function skillfully.

Ecological. A perspective that focuses on the interaction of people and environments.

Empirical. Knowledge based on direct observation or gained through the scientific method.

Empowerment. Strengthening the ability of people to achieve control of their own lives.

Generalist. A professional helper who addresses the needs of the whole person and tries to find the package of resources that will address the range of needs that people have.

Generalist social work practice. Social work that focuses on the interactions between people and the institutions of society that affect the ability of people to accomplish life tasks, realize aspirations and values, and alleviate distress.

Habilitation. A model of intervention that emphasizes education and skill development.

Helping activities. Specific behaviors performed by professional helpers that make the competencies operational on a day-to-day basis.

Holistic view of human behavior. A person-in-situation view that sees human behavior as the result of complex interactions among biological, psychological, social-structural, and cultural factors.

Specialist. A professional helper who provides specific kinds of helping services in particular types of situations.

STUDY QUESTIONS

1. Compare the biomedical (medical) and the health models in Table 1 with the habilitation and rehabilitation models in Table 2. What similarities do you see? What differences?

2. What is meant by an *ecological perspective* on human behavior? Why is such an approach helpful to the generalist social work practitioner?

3. You have probably taken a course in sociology or psychology or biology; perhaps you have even taken a course in social science research methods. In any of these courses, you would have talked about the scientific method. What limitations are there in using this method to understand human behavior? What kind of behavior is most readily understood empirically and what kind is most difficult to understand using this approach?

4. Review the purposes of social work discussed in this chapter. For each purpose, list as many concepts or theories known to you that you think would be relevant to carrying out that purpose. For example, developing people's coping capacities might entail understanding their personality, coping patterns they learned in the family as they grew up, whether they are married and employed, their culture, and so on.

5. Read Exhibit 1 at the end of this chapter. Then try to identify the knowledge needed to adequately understand April from a person-in-situation perspective. Go on to explore the knowledge needed to intervene in April's situation. Was anyone in this case functioning as a generalist?

6. Apply the Developmental Assessment Wheel to yourself. If it was utilized thoroughly would it help someone to understand the most significant aspects of you as a person, and your current situation? Explain why or why not.

REFERENCES

Baer, B. and R. Federico (1978). *Educating the Baccalaureate Social Worker,* Vol. 1. Cambridge, MA: Ballinger.

Barker, R. (1987). *The Social Work Dictionary.* Silver Spring, MD: National Association of Social Workers.

Berelson, B. and G. Steiner (1964). *Human Behavior: An Inventory of Scientific Findings.* New York: Harcourt Brace Jovanovich.

Campbell, J. (1986). *The Inner Reaches of Outer Space.* New York: Harper & Row.

Federico, R. (1990). *Social Welfare in Today's World.* New York: McGraw-Hill.

Frankl, V. (1959). *Man's Search for Meaning: An Introduction to Logotherapy.* New York: Washington Square Press.

Germain, C. and A. Gitterman (1986). The Life Model Approach to Social Work Practice Revisited. In F. Turner, ed., *Social Work Treatment: Interlocking Theoretical Approaches,* 3rd ed. New York: Free Press, pp. 618–643.

Grenier, G. (1988). *Inhuman Relations: Quality Circles and Anti-Unionism in American Industry.* Philadelphia: Temple University Press.

Hartman, A. and J. Laird (1983). *Family Centered Social Work Practice.* New York: Free Press.

Imre, R. W. (1984). The Nature of Knowledge in Social Work. *Social Work,* Vol. 29, No. 1, pp. 41–45.

Jung, C. (1968). *Analytical Psychology: Its Theory and Practice.* New York: Vintage Books.

Kagel, J. and C. Cowger (1984). Blaming the Client: Implicit Agenda in Practice Research? *Social Work,* Vol. 29, No. 4 (July–August), pp. 347–351.

Pardek, J. (1988). An Ecological Approach to Social Work Practice. *Journal of Sociology and Social Welfare*, Vol. XV, No. 2, pp. 133–145.

Parsons, R., with S. Hernandez and J. Jorgensen (1988). Integrated Practice: A Framework for Problem Solving. *Social Work*, Vol. 33, No. 5, pp. 417–421.

Polanyi, M. (1958). *The Study of Man*. Chicago: University of Chicago Press.

Schorr, L. B., with D. Schorr (1988). *Within Our Reach: Breaking the Cycle of Disadvantage*. New York: Anchor Books, p. xxiii.

Smalley, R. (1967). *Theory for Social Work Practice*. New York: Columbia University Press.

Vigilante, F. and M. Mailick (1988). Needs Resource Evaluation in the Assessment Process. *Social Work*, Vol. 33, No. 2, pp. 101–104.

Weick, A. (1986). The Philosophical Context of a Health Model of Social Work. *Social Casework*, Vol. 67, No. 9, pp. 551–559.

Wells, C. C. (1989). *Social Work Day-to-Day*, 2nd ed. White Plains, NY: Longman.

Zimbalist, S. (1977). *Historic Themes and Landmarks in Social Welfare Research*. New York: Harper & Row.

Zuboff, S. (1988). *In the Age of the Smart Machine: The Future of Work and Power*. New York: Basic Books.

EXHIBIT 1   *RUNNING AWAY: THE CASE OF APRIL SAVINO*

This case is excerpted from "Running Away" by Dennis Hevesi, New York Times Magazine, *October 2, 1988. Copyright © 1988 by The New York Times Company. Reprinted by permission.*

The tragedy of April Savino's abbreviated life is that when she finally found a home it was among the homeless—on the benches and in the bleak recesses of Grand Central Terminal. There, at last, she felt needed and even, by the strange code of the streets, respected.

To the old women with sores on their legs, walking with canes, she was an angel who fed them sandwiches and covered them with blankets. To other teenagers, she was "a wildcat" who "wouldn't take nothing from nobody."

April Savino was 15 years old when she became another of those children who live, by their whims and wits, in and around Grand Central. There, she finally felt free—from the ordeal of living in a broken home, from the frenzy of a psychiatric ward, from the constraints of residential treatment facilities.

But Grand Central is no home. For those who are not just passing through, it is, ultimately, a hellish pit of violence, drugs and despair. Fourteen months ago, April Savino sat down on the steps of a church, half a block from the terminal, and put a bullet through her head.

There are approximately 1.2 million runaway and so-called "throw-away" children in the nation, according to June Bucy, the executive director of the National Network of Runaway and Youth Services in Washington. . . .

Unlike many of the other youths in Grand Central, April had a lot going for her. Her parents, both beauticians, were not poor—not rich, but not poor. Her grandmother obviously cared about her. And April—a slim, 5-foot-6-inch, pug-nosed brunette—was intelligent, pretty and quick-witted. . . .

Many people came in contact with April, including some people of power and influence. Many tried to assist her. Could not someone, some agency, have done something to alter the course of her seemingly inexorable destruction? In many ways, April chose the way she lived; she chose to stay in the terminal. But that's too simple; she was a victim. . . .

April Candy Savino was born on July 27, 1968, the second child of Karin and Michael Savino of Fresh Meadows, Queens. "They were good parents," insists April's grandmother, Frances Savino, who lives in the Coney Island section of Brooklyn. "The kids were their life." In 1972, when April was 4 and her brother, Rodney, was 7, the Savinos moved to California. . . .

Six months after the Savinos settled in Tarzana, California, the marriage collapsed. "He left a note," Karin Savino recalls. "It said he'd come home once a year or once a month and I'd have to live with that. So I packed up and took April on the bus to New York." . . .

"They started with drugs when they went to California," Frances Savino says of her son and daughter-in-law. "I would say drugs were the start. Once they were on the dope, they couldn't handle things right. . . ."

When [the mother] got on the bus with April, she left Rodney with a cousin in California. Within weeks of her return to Queens, she had a job as a beautician. And within a few months, she had opened her own beauty parlor in Fresh Meadows. "Instead of an apartment, I rented a store," she says. One day, her husband called and announced, "Your son is at the airport, pick him up." For several months, Mrs. Savino and the children slept in the store on air mattresses.

The business prospered, and within a year, she and her children were living in . . . an expensive apartment complex. . . . The children attended [public school] and did well, according to their mother. But when April was in third grade, she recalls, "they started to complain that she lost her temper, that she threw chairs. She was immature. Her father wasn't around. I felt I had to show her I loved her more. I sent her to private school". . . .

"She was 9 when her grandfather died," April's grandmother remembers . . . "He was an idol to her. She was born on his birthday. And he was more affectionate than me. She was very hurt because she couldn't go to the funeral. None of the grandchildren were allowed to go.

"When we came back from the cemetery, April stood with a pad and pencil and took everybody's name at the table—the aunts, the cousins. She wanted to know who they were and who she was to them. She wanted family. Unfortunately, she wasn't getting it."

In 1978, April's brother, Rodney, moved back to California to live with his father. It was another loss for April. "The children were very close," according to April's grandmother. Real problems began when April was 12 and visited her father and brother.

"I couldn't postpone her any more," says Karin Savino. "She wanted to know her father. She pushed the issue. For a while, I said I don't know his phone number, because I knew he didn't want her." Eventually he relented. "Michael told me he would let her come for one week, if I paid for it."

Michael Savino had remarried. "They had a wonderful time at the Big Sur," April's grandmother says, "and when April came home she'd brag about the things her father and his wife did. It made the mother angry."

After that week in California, Karin Savino says, "it was a complete turnaround. Everything I did was bad. I was stupid. Her whole personality was negative. She wanted to go outside late at night, hang out at the pizza place. She disappeared for three, four days."

Finally, there was an explosion. "When she came at me," Mrs. Savino said, "the knife was an inch from my face. I ducked. She threw the TV at me and screamed, 'What are you gonna do now?' Eventually, I got exhausted. I sent her to Elmhurst."

On Oct. 31, 1981, April was committed to the psychiatric ward at the City Hospital Center in Elmhurst, Queens. When Frances Savino visited her granddaughter, "April was medicated, very quiet. There were kids there, screaming, yelling. She'd say, 'I'm crazy. You know I'm crazy. That's why I'm here.' I'd say, 'Don't talk like that.' "

April spent two months on the psychiatric ward. It was the start of three years during which she bounced between the hospital, her home [and various other residential treatment facilities].

At 3:30 A.M. on October 17, 1982, a car driven by Rodney Savino ran off the shoulder of Interstate Highway 15, south of Barstow, California. Rodney died of head injuries two days later. He was 17.

"It was a bad turning point," April's grandmother says. "She would talk to Rodney after he was dead." April's mother agrees: "She didn't want to live after her brother died. She was fascinated with anybody who died."

Young people like April, who get overwhelmed by stress, "feel they're entitled to be destructive to themselves or others," [a therapist speculates]. "They may have been subject to a subtle form of exploitation that results from some parents' inability or unwillingness to parent them. It destroys a kid's foundation of trust. . . .

"It is significant," [the therapist continues], "that April winds up in Grand Central Station mothering everybody, when what she so desperately needed was that kind of parenting."

[A railroad policeman who knew April when she lived at the railroad terminal recalled], "The old women with the sores and the canes, they couldn't get the food" [from the food trucks that came to feed the homeless]. "She would bring it to them, open the wrappers for them. She'd get blankets, cover them over. She was like a spark. She got all the old women laughing, brought a little life to a dreary place."

[Being attractive and articulate, April was interviewed by the media seeking stories about the homeless.] In an interview on the "CBS Evening News with Dan Rather" in March 1986, she declared: "I want a big house, one as big as this one. I'm going to marry a rich man."

Several times, April tried to assume a normal life with her grandmother in Coney Island. "First mistake is I registered her in school," recalls Frances Savino. "I wanted to treat her as a child should be treated. She said, 'Look, Grandma, I really want to go back to Grand Central. I don't want to go to school.' I didn't realize that she hadn't been to school since seventh grade. And all those kids had all those nice clothes."

Mrs. Savino owned two sets of jewelry—some costume jewelry from Mexico and "the good stuff." April stole the costume jewelry and pawned it for a few dollars. "I didn't think that she could steal."

Eventually, Mrs. Savino says, "I couldn't handle her no more." April left.

A few weeks later, Frances Savino went to Grand Central to see how her granddaughter was getting along. "I followed her. She got very nasty." April's mother also sought out her daughter at the terminal. "Sure, I said come home, but she wasn't going to come," Karin Savino says. "I didn't want to lecture. At this point, she was big; she'll belt me one. . . ."

[A friend of April's father asked him if he should visit April when he was in New York on business.] "He said, 'Well, if you're around there, look her up.' I must say, he thought it was incredibly cool that she was living there, sort of a chip off the old block." When he went to the terminal, "I saw this girl that looked like Rodney's twin. I said, 'You're April?' She says, 'Who's asking?' I told her and she asked, 'Did my father send you?' I said, 'In a manner of speaking.'

"We sat and talked for an hour. We talked about Rodney, and she cried. Then she got angry with herself for crying."

Over the next two years [the friend] went to see April about once a month. . . .

Several times . . . he offered to fly April out to California. "She would say, 'Does my father want me there?' I told her, call and ask him." On one occasion, [he] thought April was in such bad shape that he called Michael Savino himself. "He got very angry, told me I was meddling. He said, in fact, if I brought April to

California, whatever happened to her would be on my hands. I thought that was cold, because she was desperate.''

''She would say, 'That's my father.' I think she loved him very much and needed him and she wanted him to ask. He just never asked.''

After his daughter's funeral, Michael Savino was interviewed by CBS News. ''I told her that she's in something that's very, very difficult to get out of,'' he told the [CBS] reporter. ''And she said that she'd like to get out of it but didn't know how to get out of it. And I didn't know how to get her out of it. I didn't offer her to live with me. I didn't feel I could give her what she needed or what I thought she needed.''

No one, it seemed, could give April what she needed. . . .

Frances Savino wonders whether someone—someone besides herself or April's parents—couldn't have helped. ''I'm not blaming,'' she insists, ''but I really feel that all these times she was picked up they really let her slip through. . . . When Gabe Pressman [local NBC reporter] interviewed her, the other press guys—was it just a story for them?''

CHAPTER 2

The Dimensions
of Human Behavior

There are more things in heaven and earth, Horatio, than will ever be dreamed of in your philosophy.

Shakespeare

Man is an organism with certain desires existing in an environment which fails to satisfy them fully. His theories about the universe are attempts, whether religious, scientific, philosophical, or political, to explain or overcome his tension. If we regard the environment as static, then the problem is one of modifying our desires; if we take the organism as static, one of modifying the environment. Religion and psychology begin with the first; science and politics with the second.

W. H. Auden

CHAPTER OVERVIEW

Shakespeare and Auden indicate the breadth of factors that influence human behavior, as well as the creative thinking needed to comprehend the complexity of people's lives. In this chapter we will try systematically to review major concepts from the biological, behavioral, and social sciences that help practitioners to identify the parameters of the human behavior with which they work each day.

The existing body of knowledge in the many disciplines from which social work draws seems at times frightfully incomplete and inconsistent. This makes the task of selecting relevant material a difficult and confusing one. Informed intervention based on data supported by research remains the ideal condition.

The urgency of the professional task, however, presents the practitioner with a dilemma. Withholding action until all the research is completed may suggest "fiddling while Rome burns," while planning an intervention without conceptual clarity grounded in carefully executed research may be professionally irresponsible. Caught in this less than ideal situation, practitioners must make the best use of the information that is available.

This chapter will focus on the knowledge that is currently available and that we believe will help in efforts to unravel the complexities of human behavior. It will present a brief overview of concepts from the biological, behavioral, and social sciences. You will probably have already studied many of these concepts in courses that you have taken in disciplines like sociology, psychology, biology, anthropology, economics, and political science. An extended essay called "Helping and Hating the Homeless" at the end of the chapter is offered to illustrate further the multiple sources from which human behavior springs, and to serve as a stimulus for further discussion.

MASTERY, INTEGRATION, AND APPLICATION

Knowledge about human behavior that guides practice can be ordered on the empirical-philosophical dimension and the generalist-specialist continuum presented in the preceding chapter. However, practitioners also distinguish between *explanatory* and *intervention* knowledge.

Explanatory knowledge seeks only to explain a phenomenon, not to change or alter it. The academic disciplines generally seek this kind of knowledge in pursuit of their primary goal: to explain and/or predict human behavior. Applied disciplines like social work do not have as their main focus the explanation of behavior. Rather, these disciplines wish to be able to explain behavior and to intervene and change it. They seek **intervention knowledge** that is usable to influence or change human behavior.

Both types of knowledge are useful in practice. Explanatory knowledge guides the professional in answering "why" questions: Why are some people more likely to become drug or alcohol addicted than others? Why do some communities organize to expel the homeless, while others organize to help them? Why are many social welfare benefits so low that they force recipients to continue living in poverty?

Intervention knowledge is called upon in addressing "how" and "what" questions. It is integrated with explanatory knowledge and prior experience so that change becomes possible. How can self-help groups be organized to help people who are drug or alcohol addicted? What groups in a community need to be mobilized so that the needs of the homeless can be met effectively? How can policies be developed so that financial aid benefits supplement work income, thereby lifting people out of poverty? The human-service professional has a societal mandate not only to understand the human condition, a task shared with academics, but also is expected to use that understanding in a disciplined and planned way to influence and change behavior.

In addition to working together for the practitioner, explanatory and intervention knowledge are also closely related for research purposes. Issues that arise from practice situations (intervention) often become the questions upon which future research (explanation) builds. The relationship between knowledge and practice is a reciprocal one. The application of existing knowledge in practice often yields a measure of its accuracy and can serve to identify gaps and weaknesses in our existing knowledge. In return, existing knowledge directs and informs intervention and helps assess why such efforts were or were not helpful.

Knowledge shapes and focuses the helping professional's understanding of human behavior and the social environment in three interrelated and cumulative ways:

1. *Mastery*. Knowledge of biological, social, and behavioral science concepts helps to explain the multifaceted dimensions of individual, group, and social-structural behavior. These concepts come from human biology, anthropology, economics, political science, psychology, and sociology.
2. *Integration*. A holistic view of human behavior results from the integration of concepts from the multiple sources noted above.
3. *Application*. Identifying concepts with particular utility for practice enables integrated knowledge to be applied to concrete situations as part of practice and guides intervention efforts.

The interrelated and cumulative tasks of mastery, integration, and application give form and substance to the professional's understanding of the dimensions of human behavior. They become steps through which knowledge about the biological, psychological, cultural, and social-structural bases of behavior directs practice activities.

The following example will illustrate why professionals need to integrate knowledge from diverse sources to intervene effectively.

Mai is a widowed 63-year-old Vietnamese woman who came to the United States in 1987. She lives with her daughter and two teenage grandchildren. Her son-in-law was unable to leave Vietnam. Her daughter took her to the neighborhood health clinic concerned about withdrawal from the family except for intermittent outbursts of anger. Mai told her daughter that she found a lump on her breast several weeks earlier but was fearful of discussing it with anyone or seeking treatment. She was also worried about the cost of such treatment. Upon first recognizing the lump she attempted using herbal tonics and balms in hopes that it would go away. Her daughter finally was able to convince her to seek medical attention.

This vignette points to the importance of the practitioner being knowledgeable about the interrelated aspects of Mai's situation in order to make an accurate assessment of the issues and intervene in an effective and informed manner. Consider the following dimensions that influence Mai's situation: biological (age, gender, physical symptomatology); psychological (fears about treatment and its cost; anxieties about disfigurement; coping strategies); cultural (beliefs about the use of medicine; the meaning of illness, suffering, and healing); and social-structural (the lack of an adult male in the family unit who might be expected to help with such crises; the impact of illness on the family and the community; the availability of culturally acceptable medical treatment; access to resources to pay for treatment).

These are all important aspects that need to be considered in making an accurate assessment. To separate one from another would be artificial. Mai's withdrawal from the family and her seemingly uncontrollable outbursts of anger could be a manifestation of her physical illness or they could result from her fears about an illness she suspects is serious and fears is terminal. The services of several specialists, including a physician, an X-ray technician, a nutritionist, and a nurse might well be called upon as part of the assessment package. A psychologist could help to explore the impact of the recent move to a new and strange society and the lack of a respected male figure in the household. Of particular help would be advice from Vietnamese professionals who could comment on the cultural dimensions of the recent changes in Mai's life. The social worker in this case would need to pull together all of the information available from the diverse sources to make an informed assessment and know when and how to intervene on Mai's behalf.

FOUR SOURCES OF BEHAVIOR

This book will focus on four principal sources of behavior: biological, psychological, social-structural, and cultural (including spiritual). As we will see later, the value of these sources of behavior is in their interaction so that practitioners get a holistic view of the situations with which they work. For now, though, let us take a broad view of each of these sources of behavior.

Biological

Part of human behavior is biologically determined, deriving from the genetic inheritance that establishes both potentials and limits upon a person's behavior. The current literature of both the social and biological sciences is replete with arguments as to the relative influence of genetics on behavior. Indeed, sociobiologists contend that all social behavior can be explained genetically. While the controversy over "nature versus nurture" will be ongoing, we know that both play a part in human behavior: genetics and the social environment are both important.

Let us look at the behavior of an infant. It will automatically grasp and move its limbs because of species **reflexes** (reflexes are genetically programmed predispositions). The sucking reflex, however, may not be present in an infant who has a genetic disorder that causes brain damage. In some cases these innate deficits can be compensated for through learning, whereas in others the possibilities for remedy may be limited. Potentials for behavior are biologically created, but in humans certain social conditions are usually needed for them to be realized. While a brain-damaged child may be able to move its limbs only rarely because of an organic deficit, a child who is not brain damaged may move its limbs only rarely because of lack of stimulation from others. Although the behavioral results are similar in both cases, the cause is biological in one and social in the other. This underlines the importance of the interaction of biological and social-structural forces. One recent study demonstrated the powerful influences of heredity on behavior and paradoxically concludes the importance of environment as a co-determinant, energizing the continued nature (heredity)–nurture (environment) controversy (Plomin, 1989).

Biological potential is influenced by the cultural context in which it occurs, as well as by psychological and social-structural variables. Awareness of the interrelationship of these variables is translated into practice in infant stimulation programs, maternal and child-care programs, and various nutritional programs for pregnant women and young children. Such programs recognize that the realization of genetic potential is influenced by such nonbiological factors as the psychological well-being of the caretaker and the social conditions that affect whether needed environmental resources are available.

Technological sophistication brought about by computerization has also affected biological functioning by making possible the early identification of genetically "at-risk" populations. Emerging roles for helping professions in areas such as genetic counseling lend further support to the idea that technology has begun to control what in the not-so-distant past was seen as biologically predetermined.

Midlife serves as another point on the biological continuum from birth to death when one finds dramatic evidence of cultural and social-structural variables influencing biological events. Knowledge about metabolic changes accompanying midlife is explored in the biological sciences. Such changes may include hormonal secretions, alterations in various organ systems, or degenerative changes that increase vulnerability to illness and organ dysfunction. Significance is added when the psychosocial aspects of midlife are examined. The doubts and conflicts often accompanying those physical changes (the biological dimension of behavior) take form in highly personal ways. As a result, an understanding of the life experiences of people and their perceived meaning is needed (the psychological dimension of behavior). Social-structural and cultural dimensions are added when the beliefs that cultures perpetuate about midlife are examined, and when the resources or obstacles encountered as one progresses through this life stage are analyzed. People in midlife commonly report confronting their mortality and asking fundamental questions about the meaning of life (the spiritual dimension) (Carlson, 1988).

The novelist David Leavitt (1989) offers a powerful example of the interaction of these multiple sources of behavior. In an article in which he discusses his personal struggle to overcome ignorance and denial about AIDS, he points out how the media consistently refer to children and people who contracted the disease through blood transfusions as "innocent victims," implying that gay men and intravenous drug users are somehow "guilty victims." His examples demonstrate how AIDS (biological) is differentially handled as it filters through societal prejudices (cultural) toward homosexual men and intravenous drug users. Prejudices such as these often become institutionalized in discriminatory public policies (sociocultural) and sometimes become internalized (psychological) by the populations they exploit. Leavitt further shows how people with AIDS have successfully overcome many of these negative cultural definitions through political action (socio-structural).

Psychological

A second source of behavior is psychological, resulting from people's perception, cognition, and emotional development. The human species is unique in that the amount of the behavior controlled by reflexes is limited. Much of what we can do we have learned through the use of biological/psychological potential. Human behavior is made operational through the development of perceptual, cognitive, and motor capacities, as well as through the development of personality structures that mediate between individual needs and the social-structural environment. The development of psychological components is heavily dependent on human interaction—the process of individuals relating to each other in supportive, competitive, or even destructive ways. Once psychological capacities are developed they become important determinants of the behavior of individuals and groups.

Psychological growth and development, like biological functioning, does not exist in a vacuum. It is responsive to the cultural and socio-structural context in which it occurs. Developing a positive self-image, for example, is supported by an environment that applauds one's efforts and provides the resources (interpersonal and financial) to accelerate the accomplishment of one's goals. The social-structural climate, however, could just as easily present obstacles to building a positive self-concept. Ageism, racism, sexism, and homophobia are examples of some of the powerful ways the cultural matrix impacts on one's sense of self-worth. Some elderly people, for example, have a seriously damaged self-concept as a result of having internalized society's negative stereotypes about old age. Societal supports have crumbled and a series of losses have ensued—less income, reduced capacity for physical functioning, and restricted social roles. Some programs attempt to at least partially reverse this downward spiral. The congregate meal program (a social-structural arrangement that brings elderly people together for shared meals), which is part of the Older Americans Act, acknowledges the interrelationship between the necessity for programs that meet nutritional (biological) needs and the need to provide opportunities for socializing with others (psychological). This service attempts to reduce both nutritional deficiency and social isolation, thereby recognizing how closely intertwined these sources of behavior are.

Social-Structural

Social structures represent a third source of behavior. **Social structures,** such as the family, the church, schools, and the economic system, exist to organize and pattern social interaction. This is important for social order, making it possible for people to behave with some degree of predictability. A sense of order is also generally perceived by people as reassuring and helpful in guiding their personal goals and behaviors. However, once structures exist, they control behavior and exert pressure to maintain themselves. These pressures have to be balanced with the individual needs that these structures are meant to serve. For example, social agencies are created to serve those in need, but these agencies may become so rigid in the creation and application of rules that services become ineffective. The issue of balancing individual and societal needs is ever-present in human life and is inevitable given the fact that humans depend primarily on social interaction rather than on genetically programmed behavior.

You may find it more difficult to understand the impact of socio-structural variables on human behavior than biological or psychological influences. This is partly due to the abstract nature of social structures: it is impossible to "touch" a social institution like the family, for instance, although most of us have been raised in a particular family. But the difficulty also stems from the persistent cultural belief that the individual can overcome environmental deficiencies through the development of a strong character. Explicating the impact of social-structural arrangements on biological and psychological developments becomes one of the goals of studying human behavior and the social environment. Socio-structural determinants of behavior demand focusing not only on the family but also on the programs, policies, and services that employ and pay us, and the political structures that govern and control us. People are treated differently based on their position in the social structure and the resources available to them.

Many of the social problems plaguing the United States are rooted in social-structural arrangements that benefit some groups at the expense of others. Gans (1971) points out how poverty serves the needs of the non-poor, for instance, in that it creates employment for social workers, provides workers who will work for low pay at undesirable jobs, gives the leisure classes a tax-deductible charitable contribution, and maintains a pool of people to populate slum housing. Addressing the problems of poverty, according to Gans's analysis, necessitates major institutional change, including finding a better power balance between the poor and the non-poor. The idea of changing individuals is easier for most of us to entertain than the idea of changing society. The tendency for outmoded and unjust social structures to perpetuate themselves speaks to their resiliency.

Cultural

All human behavior occurs within a cultural context. **Culture** embodies the values, knowledge, and material technology that people learn to accept as appropriate and desirable. Therefore, culture establishes the parameters that guide and often limit people's thinking and behavior. Culture represents human-kind's master plan; it molds our way of explaining the world and charts the limits of allowable behavior. Its influence on human action takes on added significance in a society composed of many cultural groups. The United States, for example, is made up of a diverse range of ethnic, socioeconomic, and lifestyle groups, each of which influences the thinking and behavior of its members. Because one person may belong to several cultural groups simultaneously—Roman Catholic, single parent, Italian-American, female with few economic resources—each cultural influence on behavior may be subtle and diverse. These influences become even more complex given the need to create a viable culture that integrates many disparate groups.

As with socio-structural influences on behavior, cultural influences are seldom directly observable, at least to the untrained eye. Their effects, however, are nonetheless powerful and pervasive. The individual is rarely conscious of the role culture plays in determining behavior, and cultural practices become so habitual that we often think of them as "natural." For example, we may consider it "natural" for women to shave their legs and armpits, and unnatural for men (except swimmers or dancers, perhaps) to do likewise. Conforming to cultural stereotypes eliminates many of the individual decisions one must make in any given day, and thus conformity accounts for much of the predictability in human behavior. Challenging stereotypes, on the other hand, often results in negative sanctions. Culture guides and instructs human beings in much the same way that instincts guide other animal species. At several levels, then, culture is an important source of behavior.

Spirituality is one component of the cultural dimension that deserves special mention. It is important not to confuse spirituality, however, with religion, an element of the social structure. Joseph Campbell (1988) views spirituality as the universal calling to a deeper awareness of oneself and of one's connectedness to others as well as the quest to understand what lies beyond the visible world. Herbert Miller (1970) notes that people look to the humanities to answer "how shall we live, and what shall we do?'' questions. While these kinds of inquiries do not lend themselves easily to answers through the use of scientific methodology, they nonetheless serve as powerful motivators of human behavior. Discounting the impact of spirituality as a dimension that shapes human behavior would be like ignoring magnetism as a force in the physical world because we cannot see it. Many people view spirituality as irrational and therefore meaningless, whereas others see it as a source of both individual and collective nourishment. As a practitioner committed to viewing the person holistically, the social worker needs to be aware of spirituality as a component that is helpful in understanding the total person. Think, for instance, of the mother of a child dying from gunshots fired during a shooting spree in a fast-food restaurant. She struggles to make sense of this tragic event, wondering why it has happened. When the child dies, spirituality is part of her coping to help her through the grieving process.

While it is possible to analyze the four sources of behavior separately, in reality they work together to shape human life. Each human being has a unique biological endowment that creates his or her behavior potentials. The degree to which this potential is realized, however, is heavily influenced by our culture, our psychological development, and our social-structural environment. For example, a woman who is born with the potential for high intellectual achievement but who lives in a culture that does not value intelligence in women is unlikely to have many opportunities to develop her intellectual capacities to their fullest potential. If, for instance, her family values intellectual achievement and has sufficient economic resources, it may help her to take advantage of the educational resources society provides. If, on the other hand, the family's values concur with the culture's devaluation of education for women, or if the family lacks the economic resources needed to finance an education, the woman will most likely have few opportunities to develop her biological intellectual potential. Indeed, in such a situation she may even begin to think of herself as unintelligent or deviant if others treat her as such.

These examples illustrate that it is the interaction of biological, social-structural, psychological, and cultural sources of behavior that most often proves significant in determining an individual's life experience. Any one of them viewed in isolation is far less influential than when viewed in interaction with the others.

UNDERSTANDING THE SOURCES
OF BEHAVIOR: BASIC CONCEPTS

An understanding of the four sources of behavior depends on mastery of the basic concepts that describe and explain specific components of behavior. These concepts are generated and codified in the major social, biological, and behavioral science disciplines, most importantly human biology, psychology, sociology, anthropology, political science, economics, and in the fine arts and the humanities. You may have already studied some or all of these disciplines and may have been introduced to their most important concepts, or you may be in the process of doing so. It is important to study concepts in the context of their respective disciplines. This provides the historical and methodological perspectives needed to understand them fully in all their richness.

The remainder of this chapter reviews many of the major concepts needed to understand the four sources of behavior. This review is for the purpose of ensuring your knowledge of the individual concepts so that you can use them in various combinations dictated by the need to view helping situations in a holistic way. Later chapters in the book will help you to combine concepts. While the following summary of concepts will provide a useful common base for the rest of the text, three cautions should be observed:

1. There is no substitute for the level of understanding gained from studying these concepts in their respective disciplines.
2. This summary is selective. The concepts presented are only a representation of those that are potentially useful in professional practice. You should be constantly alert to others that may also be useful.
3. Resist fragmentation of concepts and remember that human life is a complex whole. The concepts discussed in one area, such as the biological source of behavior, frequently have applicability in other areas as well.

To avoid a random listing, concepts will be organized under the familiar headings of biological, psychological, social-structural, and cultural. It is hoped that this four-part framework will prove to be convenient and manageable. Before beginning, remember that this is only a selection of very briefly summarized concepts.

Basic Concepts from Human Biology

The most fundamental concept of human behavior is **life** itself. *The physiological process of life is the management of complex chemical processes mediated by the brain through an elaborate series of neurological impulses.* The brain serves as a command center that activates (or fails to activate) the chemical substances and their interactions that begin at conception. At conception, a female egg is fertilized by a male sperm. The union combines genetic information from the two parents in the form of 46 chromosomes, which then chart the newly conceived individual's biological potential. Each combination of genetic information is multigenerational as well as unique. It is multigenerational in that the parents carry genetic information from their parents, which may in turn be passed on to the newly conceived generation. This is true even for genetic information that is not physically evident in the parent as, for example, when red-haired children are born to parents neither of whom have red hair.

Genetic combinations are unique in that a mixing process occurs during fertilization so that only some genetic elements of each parent become part of the newly created fetus. Recent discoveries have modified earlier thinking about genetics. Human cells contain 23 chromosome pairs, with one in each pair thought to come from the mother and the other from the father. However, instances have now been found where both chromosomes in a pair have come from the same parent. In addition, it has been discovered that genes may behave differently depending on whether they came from the mother or the father (*Science News*, 1989). These discoveries derive from research seeking to find ways to modify genetic material so as to prevent or cure physiologically based problems. The modification of genetic material is called **genetic engineering**.

Another influence acting on the usual pattern of gene transmission is that of **mutation**, a process in which genes are changed from their original form when they are transmitted at conception. While mutations are relatively rare, they and the natural genetic mixing process that occurs at conception ensure human differences. Thus, a person's genetic inheritance becomes an important basis for his or her social uniqueness, because social development depends upon the potentials created by genetic inheritance.

Because of this genetically defined potential for behavior, human beings have tremendous adaptive potential. Rather than being guided primarily by genetically programmed reflexes that predispose the organism to react in set ways to particular situations, humans can make use of many types of resources in many different ways. For example, nutritional needs are met by utilizing a variety of plant and animal substances. Humans also can learn how to process potential nutrients so that they can be better digested through curing processes, cooking, and storage strategies to avoid spoilage, to name a few. This flexibility makes it possible for humans to adapt to any number of geographical and climatic environments, thus demonstrating how far-reaching genetic flexibility is in humans.

It is the complex interplay of chemical digestive processes, brain development and functioning capacity, and skeletal-muscular potential that makes humans so adaptable. All of these factors are part of the genetic potential that humans as a species inherit, although each individual has a unique set of particular potentials and limitations. As will be discussed later, part of the human inheritance is the potential for language, which makes culture possible. The interaction of culture and biology then becomes extremely important in human behavior by preserving and transmitting those types of adaptations that have proven most effective.

Once created, life must be actively sustained or it will quickly end. Part of the human's genetic inheritance is a set of instructions that cause physiological growth and development to occur in an orderly process throughout the **life span**, which is the period of life from conception to death. When the genetic plan is able to unfold because the resources needed to permit growth and development have been provided, we can talk about **physiological health**. As noted earlier, the genetic plan can accommodate extensive variation and adaptation while moving the human organism through the stages of increasing size, complexity, and autonomy that characterize growth and development.

In a state of health, there is relatively stable interaction and exchange among the various components of the human body. For example, enough blood is pumped by the heart and adequately oxygenated by the lungs to feed the muscles so that they contract and relax in the process of use that leads to their increase in size and strength. This view of the human body is a systemic one, focusing on the way the parts (organs, bones, muscles, blood, nerves, and so on) of a whole (the biological body) work together to allow the whole to maintain itself in its environment. The maintenance of a relatively steady state of a system is called **homeostasis**. Obviously, the concept of systems is a complex one (others include the family, the community, society, and so on). In Chapter 3, systems will be analyzed in more detail.

Because the end of life is part of the life span, **degenerative processes** are part of the developmental process. As the human body ages, the genetic plan begins to enact the deterioration of cells at a rate and in a pattern unique to each person. Degenerative processes are strongly affected by stress, which pushes a person toward or beyond her or his adaptive capacity. Stress may occur at any point in the life span and is often experienced in the form of inadequate **nutrition**, which is a lack of the basic nutrients needed for physiological health; inadequate **nurturance**, or lack of the basic protection and caring needed for psychological well-being, which strongly affects physiological health; and an environment that lacks basic life-sustaining and life-enriching resources. Stress often generates **pain** as a warning that some part of the system is being pushed toward its adaptive limit.

There may also be a relationship between degenerative processes and *deficits*, which is defined as the potential for growth and development that may be limited, sometimes severely, by parts of the human system that are deficient or whose functioning is severely constrained. This can be due to genetic inheritance or traumas, such as accidents. Brain damage, for example, is a deficit that may affect the entire neurological structure and the ability of the brain to manage other physiological processes. The existence of major physical deficits often interacts with and accelerates the degenerative processes that are a natural part of the life cycle. Life ends in **death**, the point at which the human body is no longer able to sustain itself. Death is inevitable and is the result of genetically programmed patterns. Death may also be caused by stress that pushes the body beyond its adaptive limits—the trauma, or shock, of blood loss caused by an accident, for example.

Although conception and death are fundamentally biological processes, their significance is most often defined by the social context in which they occur. For example, the deaths of an infant, a middle-aged breadwinner, and an elderly person have very different effects on other individuals and social groups, such as family members and family units. Survivors react differently to the death of someone following a long chronic illness than they would to a sudden accidental death, or to a murder, no matter what the age of the deceased. Religious beliefs and practices associated with funeral rituals demonstrate how different cultures deal with death and mourning differently.

Now let us turn to some examples of how biological processes affect human behavior and discuss implications for social work practice. Genetic research continues to stress the influence of hereditary factors on human behavior (Snyderman and Rothman, 1987). Specific cognitive processes including verbal and spatial abilities and styles of learning have been linked to genetic factors. An individual, for instance, may possess skill in mastering foreign languages yet encounter difficulty in geometry owing to problems in conceptualizing spatial relationships. Manual dexterity and fine motor coordination have also been found to be linked to genetic factors. Someone with unusual sensitivity combined with manual dexterity may find art, drafting, or architecture congruent with his or her innate abilities. Conversely, someone lacking these skills may find attempts at mastering the same areas a frustrating experience. Combining social-structural resources and psychological support with innate capacity is essential for realizing human potential.

Research suggests that genetics may also be related to sociability throughout the life span (Plomin, 1989). This may have significant implications in practice. Mental-health professions have traditionally related infant **autism,** or severe emotional withdrawal from others, to unconscious parental rejection. Parents of these infants were traditionally viewed as in need of intensive psychotherapy. If autism is instead primarily a biological phenomenon that is genetically pro- grammed, intervention would shift from the intrapsychic realm to the social- structural arena in terms of providing parents with concrete services, education, and social support. Similar findings trace the role of genetics in such mental disorders as depression and schizophrenia (Bower, 1989; Reich and others, 1987; Schmeck, 1987).

Other areas in which genetic predispositions have been traced include alcoholism (Wallace, 1989), substance abuse, and eating disorders. It is impor- tant to underline *predisposition*. Some traits (color of eyes, color of hair, gender, etc.) are determined with little or no environmental influence. Others are par- tially determined by environmental factors. A child who has the genetic potential to be a 6-foot-5-inch guard on a basketball team may be thwarted from realizing this because of nutritional deprivation in early childhood that stunts the young- ster's growth. Research has even shown that a person's looks have a surprisingly significant impact on the way the person is perceived and treated by others

(Brody, 1981). Genetic makeup thus provides the individual with potential that can be either enhanced or thwarted by environmental factors.

Social workers need to be familiar with other biological processes that influence human behavior. Nutritional disorders such as failure to thrive and malnutrition are more likely to occur in the context of poverty. Research supports strong linkages between these disorders and cognitive and physical development (Lozoff, 1989). A disproportionate number of students from inner-city schools are diagnosed as suffering from ADD (Attention Deficient Disorder). These children are described as unable to attend to tasks as a result of an inability to block out extraneous stimuli. The provision of economic resources, improved health care, and supportive education programs may minimize the impact of the disorder.

You may find it helpful in understanding the impact of biological factors on behavior to consider the life-style changes that are often necessitated by diseases like AIDS, arthritis, asthma, diabetes, and hypertension. Individuals react differently to each of these illnesses, in part depending on the severity of the symptoms and prognosis, and in part due to individual coping styles. Yet each may affect the person's functioning ability and needs to be carefully addressed in making an assessment for intervention purposes.

The above discussion points to some of the ways biological factors influence human behavior. Beginning practitioners may find themselves in practice settings that require more specialized knowledge. A social worker in a child protective agency may need to know much more about early childhood development, parent-child bonding, and physical indicators of abuse or neglect. A worker in a multiservice center serving older adults, on the other hand, will need more specialized knowledge about the impact of physical changes on the behavior of the aging person. In all cases, the social work profession seeks to maximize biological potential, promote growth and development, and eliminate the disabling effects of illness through programs, policies, and services that support and encourage the development of all people.

Mildred Seltzer (1989), a gerontologist, in an article in which she combines personal and professional musings on the aging process, provides a poignant illustration of how the biological process of aging is influenced by cultural, psychological, and social-structural factors.

> Whose body does not speak to her or him? We may not always listen, but the clues are there. With age we begin to listen, sometimes restlessly, sometimes with interest. We need no mirror to reflect an image. Instead, the arms/eye ratio changes resulting in the need for glasses. The sound barrier is greater. The thresholds for fatigue, taste, and recuperation change. The data are reinforced by our daily experiences. Research and reality match. We have achieved, for the moment, reliability and validity. Our concepts are grounded by the lives of daily experience.

These clues result in changes in self-perception. We cannot do what we used to. Is our occasional disinterest in doing what we used to do an effort to reduce cognitive dissonance? To avoid embarrassment? Are we accepting of the changes? We begin to redefine ourselves as more vulnerable and our increasing vulnerability, in turn, results in anxiety. One is reminded of the song "Sunrise, Sunset" in [sic] "Fiddler on the Roof." The days have flown swiftly, and the body that housed that earlier "me" is heavier, more demanding, changing in how it responds to stimuli, food, and the general environment. It tells the person "I am not what I used to be" and thus forces acknowledgement at some level that "What I was is not what I am." There are benchmarks, signs, and evidence of aging, and while one is not sure when or where the processes occurred which cause these cues, signs, and evidence, it is obvious that they necessitate reappraisal of what these changes mean. Being and becoming, as Allport noted so long ago, dictate an unending process of negotiation; one waged within as well as without. (pp. 4–5)

Basic Psychological Concepts

Let us move now to an examination of some psychological concepts that are fundamental to our understanding of human behavior. People's responses to their environment are dependent on their understanding of it, which in turn is the result of psychological processes combining biological and social factors. In terms of understanding the environment, three biologically based capacities are of particular importance. **Perception** is the ability to see, smell, feel, and touch, and to develop organized responses to the sensory characteristics of the environment. The multiple stimuli that fill the natural and social environment require the capacity to perceive selectively to avoid becoming confused and overwhelmed. Residents of large cities may be more accustomed to the loud noises and fast-paced movements found there and find ways to "tune out" extraneous stimuli. Note the number of runners wearing headphones in their attempt to block out unwanted noise. Visitors, however, confronted with the same stimuli, may experience tension and confusion until they learn appropriate adaptive strategies. Through their sensory mechanisms, people receive stimuli that enable them to react to their environment for specific (often survival) purposes. Children who have been physically abused often develop heightened sensitivity to visual (fast movements) and auditory (loud voices) stimuli as a result of their constant need to monitor their environment for possible physical aggression. Vietnam veterans report that they needed to be acutely aware of danger signs provided by sight, sound, and smell in order to survive in the hostile war environment.

Cognition is the ability to process and organize information in order to utilize the environment to achieve one's goals. It involves remembering, understanding, and evaluating data. Cognitive processes are highly individualized, which partly explains why the same events are experienced by each person in a unique manner. Reactions to sensory information and events are, therefore, determined not only by the events themselves, but by the meanings the person assigns to the events (Newberger and DeVos, 1988). Stated another way, objective realities are sifted through the person's subjective interpretation of those realities. In the examples of the child-abuse survivor and Vietnam veteran cited above, sensory data have been processed cognitively so as to strengthen adaptation and coping.

Watzlawick, Weakland, and Fisch (1974) provide the following exercise to demonstrate how cognitive structures influence one's perception. Using straight lines, connect all nine dots without lifting your pencil or pen from the paper or retracing any line. The solution can be found at the end of this chapter.

```
  •     •     •


  •     •     •


  •     •     •
```

As you do this exercise, keep in mind what it teaches us about cognition. If you encountered difficulty in completing the exercise, the reason is probably because you limited yourself to unstated yet assumed rules regarding its completion. People often see the nine-dot configuration as a limited space in which all possible solutions must be contained. Memories, past experiences of similar or related tasks, and previous learning all influence how you approached the task. Our cognitive structures, in other words, have an effect on our ability to perceive spatial relationships, thereby limiting our possible solutions.

We can see, then, that the world is both an objective and a subjective reality. Our behavior is affected more by what we perceive and understand of our environment than by what actually exists. Although we all inhabit the same physical world, and share much of the same social world, we do not all perceive and organize data in the same way. Therefore, our behaviors will differ according to our cognitive processing of our environment.

Affect is the feelings and emotions that become attached to information derived from our sensory and cognitive processes. Affect involves feelings, temperament, and emotions. Think back on your attempt to solve the puzzle above. What emotions did you experience? Did you feel anxiety? Tension? Excitement? If you solved the puzzle, did you feel pride? Feelings are a result of the meanings we attach to our cognitions. Behavior, as expressed through action, is partially determined by these feelings.

Perception, cognition, and affect all have physiological roots. The workings of an eye, the functioning of a brain, the hormonal responses to a threatening situation are all examples. However, the social environment is obviously a powerful factor on the ways these biologically based capacities are developed and are used, demonstrating once again the close interaction of biological and social roots of behavior.

The flexibility with which humans are blessed because of their genetic inheritance adds another dimension to perception, cognition, and affect. The social environments in which people live attribute particular meaning to certain events and objects. These meanings are learned through the process of **socialization** through which people acquire the beliefs, customs, values, and attitudes of their culture. Through socialization we learn what we are expected to do and how we are to accomplish it. Socialization is at work when we use our cognitive capacities to learn to do some things and are relatively unconcerned about learning to do others. For example, Europeans consider it valuable to learn several languages because of the close geographical proximity of other countries, but the relative geographical isolation of the United States has tended to make this ability less of a perceived concern. We also learn what is considered to be good-looking or handsome in our culture, so the looks that will evoke deferential responses from others will vary from culture to culture.

Socialization influences our perceptions, which in turn influence the way we react to others and to situations, including the amount and type of affect (emotional investment) we accord to people, events, or objects. People perceived as important evoke feelings of affection or respect. Situations that we have learned are threatening or confusing become associated with feelings of apprehension, fear, or inadequacy. Once again we can see how our behavior is often determined more by our subjective interpretation of events than by their objective reality.

The physiological potentials for perception, cognition, and emotion become part of the individual's response to the environment. **Personality** is the integrating psychological structure that develops to help the individual function in the environment. Personality is composed of fairly consistent patterns of responses to situations, patterns that are consistent within an individual but differ from one individual to the next. Whereas some people may respond to threatening situations by running away, others respond to them with excitement. Some people express anger very directly, while others find it difficult to let people know when they are angry. In these and countless other ways, people differ in their responses to situations according to their personality characteristics.

The personality's task of mediating between the individual and the environment is closely related to the individual's needs. Some needs—for example, eating and resting—are primarily physical and do not have to be learned. Others are much more social, such as feeling secure, competent, and loved. Needs are most often learned through interaction with others and through the socialization that results. For example, while no one has to be taught to need food, we all do have to learn what foods we need in order to be healthy, the steps we need to take when preparing food, and good table manners so as to be accepted in polite company.

Efforts to better understand personality development have been going on for many years. The disciplines of psychology and sociology have presented us with several theoretical perspectives on personality development. Researchers have also studied the genetic dimensions of personality (Thompson, 1968). As in the previous section on the biological base of behavior, you will already be familiar with much of this knowledge, but you may benefit from a review. Ideas from learning theories, cognitive theories, psychoanalytic theories, and humanistic theories will be briefly discussed after a quick look at some developing biological research. No attempt has been made to provide specific citations for all of the material presented here, but a bibliography of references is included at the end of the chapter.

Biology and Personality. Recent research on twins found that the genetic make-up of children may have a surprisingly strong influence on personality development (Goleman, 1986). This challenges some of the personality theories that we shall discuss, theories that have tended to emphasize childrearing as the primary source of personality development. Much more research will be needed to clarify further the genetic role in personality development. However, the possibility of stronger genetic influences than were previously thought is a distinct possibility. This is especially so since research has in general been finding stronger than previously imagined influences of genetics on many dimensions of physiological and social functioning.

Other recent research has focused on the stability of major personality traits through the life span (Goleman, 1987). Data suggest that some traits, such as anxiety level, friendliness, and eagerness for novel experiences, remain fairly constant. Others, such as alienation, morale, and feelings of satisfaction, may vary. If additional research confirms these preliminary findings, there would be cause to rethink some of the prevailing theories about the effect of life-span stages of personality functioning.

While genetic research is getting increasingly sophisticated and raising intriguing new possibilities about personality, by far most of the research has been in the areas of psychology and sociology. We will now turn to the theories and concepts generated in these disciplines.

Learning Theories of Personality. Learning theories assume that all human behavior is reactive, meaning that specific acts have specific antecedents and so are responses to specific stimuli (Langer, 1969:51–73). Human behavior, according to this perspective, involves constant transactions between individuals and their environment. Behavior is linked to a chain of units consisting of stimulus (S) and response (R). The learning process involved is termed *conditioning*. Learning theories are supported by a wide range of research studies in which responses to stimuli were conditioned through rewards and punishments. A child who has been bitten by a dog may experience fear when the dog is seen again. The child may experience *stimulus generalization* and avoid all dogs in the future because of the original encounter. S-R reactions are, according to learning theories, at the root of all learning, whether it be the acquisition of language or the development of unique behavior mannerisms.

Albert Bandura's (1977) *social learning theory* expands the simple stimulus-response patterns of traditional learning theories to include complex issues of social interaction. Behavior, according to Bandura, involves the human person monitoring the consequences of his or her own actions to behave in a way that will produce desired outcomes. Through *imitation* and *modeling* people observe the behavior of others and develop behavioral patterns accordingly. Social learning theories emphasize the use of positive consequences rather than negative reinforcement as a central dynamic in behavioral change.

Behavioral techniques are widely used in schools and in social agencies. The emphasis placed on evaluation and measurement grounded in solid research, as well as the emphasis of the role of environmental factors in shaping behavior, partly accounts for the popularity of this group of theories with practitioners. Gambrill (1987) reports successful application of behavior modification in child welfare, family services, corrections, and in working with the elderly. However, the successful use of these techniques requires the ability to specify stimuli to which people will respond and the rewards or reinforcements that will be effective. Being able to do so depends on knowledge of social-structural and cultural variables that influence people's behaviors in specific situations.

Cognitive Theories of Personality. Cognitive theorists believe that human behavior is shaped by the manner in which the person processes information received from the environment. Whereas behavioral approaches emphasize stimulus-response and reward and reinforcement as determinants of behavior, the cognitive perspective stresses the role of thinking, imagination, creativity, emotions, and values in human action.

Jean Piaget, the most frequently cited of the cognitive theorists, explains how the child, progressing through sequentially based stages of increasing complexity, learns to respond to the environment (Langer, 1969:107–156). From birth to about 2 years of age, the infant processes information primarily through the senses and body movements. Piaget calls this the *sensorimotor stage*. The *preoperational stage* begins at about 2 years of age and extends until approximately 7 years. During this period the child processes information through his or her own actions. Unable to generalize classes of objects and events, the world is experienced in a literal way. From the ages of 7 through 11 the child begins to employ logic in assigning meaning to experience. During this stage of *concrete operations* the youngster develops the ability to classify information into categories and can begin to form simple generalizations about the world. Piaget's last developmental stage is termed *formal operations* and begins around 12 years of age. Thinking at this stage can involve imagination and complex problem solving.

From a cognitive perspective, the person sifts information from the environment through pre-existing structures called *schemas*. Maria Montessori used cognitive concepts in her theory of education and designed educational materials consistent with the child's developing capacities to interact with the environment. She believed that each child would naturally extract information from these materials according to his or her innate abilities.

Cognitive approaches are used by practitioners in explaining human behavior and in designing intervention strategies. Behavior, according to cognitive theories, is determined by the individual's thoughts, emotions, and conscious judgments based on existing information or schema. We attribute meaning to events and experiences, and we behave accordingly. The death of a casual acquaintance, for instance, will not elicit the same emotional response and consequent behavior that the death of a parent will. The anxiety generated by an upcoming quiz will not trigger the same discomfort a college entrance exam would. The events themselves, in other words, are not as significant in determining our behavior as the meanings that we attribute to them.

Cognitive restructuring is the process of applying cognitive theory to intervention and involves a conscious restructuring of the thoughts and emotions underlying dysfunctional behavior. Social workers often combine cognitive and behavioral approaches in the process of planned change. For example, psychosocial assessments from a cognitive perspective require identifying the thought patterns and beliefs that underlie problematic behaviors. Traditional social work techniques such as clarification, confrontation, and interpretation are frequently used in cognitively based intervention (Sherman, 1987).

Psychoanalytic Theories of Personality. Freud believed that human behavior was heavily influenced by unconscious processes. The unsociable person is motivated primarily by instinctual drives, according to psychoanalytic theory, and it is only through successful resolution of innate conflicts between these instinctual drives and societal constraints that passion yields to reason as a determinant of behavior (Langer, 1969:13–23).

The battle between satisfying one's own instinctual drives and the demands of others was seen by Freud as occurring through the interaction of the id, ego, and superego, the major components of the personality structure. The *id* is the part of the personality that seeks to gratify instinctual drives, whereas the *superego* is the part of the personality that incorporates the demands of society. The *ego* mediates between the id and the superego, attempting to find ways in which the needs of both can be met. *Defense mechanisms* are used by the ego as part of the mediating process, and healthy personalities result from the flexible and adaptive use of these tools.

The development of a strong and functionally adaptive ego occurs through a series of stages. Each corresponds to a specific bodily zone in which instinctual patterns are activated. The *oral stage* is the one in which the mouth is the primary source of stimulation and pleasure, and is of most significance from birth to about 1 year of age. During the *anal stage,* attention shifts to the anus, and bowel movements become the prime source of gratification or frustration (1–3 years of age). At about 3 years the child enters the *phallic stage,* in which the genital area becomes the focus of the child's instinctual drives. This lasts until about age 5. Freud believed that the child's sexual drives then became dormant and socialization took precedence during the *latency stage* (6–12 years of age). Sexual needs arose again during puberty.

Freudian theory asserts that if the child experiences too much gratification or becomes excessively frustrated in dealing with instinctual drives during a particular phase, the youngster will become fixated at that developmental stage. Each stage needs to be successfully negotiated prior to moving on to the next one. Freud did not extend his developmental model beyond puberty. However, a disciple of Freud, Erik Erikson, did extend the Freudian developmental model throughout the life span through the use of the social and cultural *matrix.*

Erikson postulated eight developmental stages, each characterized by a psychosocial crisis involving the interaction of biological, psychological, socio-structural, and cultural variables. He presents psychosocial tasks accompanying each developmental stage in terms of polar opposites. Table 3 (page 44) summarizes Erikson's developmental theory. The psychosocial tasks are presented on a continuum, reflecting the opinion that individuals function somewhere between the polarities possible for each.

Now let us look briefly at each of these stages.

1. Infancy. Infants, while born with many innate capacities to learn and interact with their environment, are unable to care for themselves. Food, warmth, touch, stimulation are all essential ingredients for the survival of the infant and for successful bonding with the caregiver. Lack of any of these "nutrients" can result in serious emotional or physical harm, including death. Resolution of this developmental stage leads to the infant's developing sense of trust that basic needs will be met. In his latest work, which focuses on the culmination of the

TABLE 3. ERIKSON'S DEVELOPMENTAL STAGES

Stage	Psychosocial Task	Successful Resolution
1. Infancy	Trust-mistrust	Hope
2. Early childhood	Autonomy-shame/doubt	Will
3. Middle childhood	Initiative-guilt	Purpose
4. Late childhood	Industry-inferiority	Competence
5. Adolescence	Identity-identity confusion	Fidelity
6. Young adulthood	Intimacy-isolation	Love
7. Maturity	Generativity-self absorption	Care
8. Old age	Integrity-despair	Wisdom

(Adapted from Erikson [1976].)

impact of each of these stages in old age, Erikson believes that the successful completion of the infancy stage results in appreciation of interdependence and relatedness (Goleman, 1988).

2. Early childhood. Toddlers experience a developing sense of independence from their caregivers. Through crawling, walking, and climbing they explore new and exciting spaces. Parents, while encouraging this emerging sense of self, need to provide safety and limits. Nowhere is this struggle more evident than in the rituals surrounding toilet training. Resolution of this stage creates a sense of autonomy and will. It culminates in old age with acceptance of the cycle of life, from integration to disintegration.

3. Middle childhood. At about 4 or 5 years of age the child begins attempts at mastery of the environment through imitating the behavior and activities of adults. Children at this stage take an active interest in activities that are physically engaging. Support of these interests encourages the development of creativity and initiative while excessive criticism may result in the child's sense that natural curiosity is bad. In old age, this stage contributes humor, empathy, and resilience.

4. Late childhood. Developing competencies in school, at home, with peers, and in social activities becomes the central concern of late childhood. If the child does not develop a sense of his or her own skill and competence during this stage, a sense of inferiority may continue throughout life. Successful completion of the tasks of this stage yields in old age humility and acceptance of the course of one's life and unfulfilled hopes.

5. Adolescence. During late adolescence the teenager must integrate several roles that appear in conflict. The roles of family member, student, friend, dating companion, and worker can create emotional strain on the adolescent. Hormonal changes accompanying emerging sexuality often find the adolescent in conflict with cultural values and belief systems. Blending these opposite demands in a manner that allows continued growth is what Erikson terms *identity*. The culmination in old age is a sense of the complexity of life, and a merger of sensory, logical, and aesthetic perception.

6. *Young adulthood.* The primary task of early adulthood is the ability to form intimate relationships with others without the fear of losing oneself. If this psychosocial task is not successfully negotiated, the individual experiences alienation and isolation. When successfully completed, in old age it results in a sense of the complexity of relationships, and the value of tenderness and loving freely.

7. *Maturity.* Adulthood again places many demands on the individual faced with negotiating many roles: spouse, lover, friend, adult child, parent, and co-worker. Adulthood is also the period when the individual becomes concerned with passing on to the next generation his or her productive and creative efforts. Parenting, teaching, and monitoring are common ways through which generativity is assured. In old age, the result is a sense of *caritas*, caring for others, and *agape*, empathy and concern.

8. *Old age.* Erikson believes the central task of old age is making sense of one's life and believing that one's having been here matters in a significant way. Successful aging involves a sense of pride in one's accomplishments and an acceptance of one's own life as well as a willingness to face one's mortality. If these late life tasks are not resolved, despair and depression characterize old age. When they are successfully accomplished, old age culminates in existential identity, with a sense of integrity strong enough to withstand physical disintegration.

Those who use the psychoanalytic approach in social work practice generally emphasize therapeutic techniques to return the client to childhood situations and emotions. These are confronted and worked through so that their effect on current behavior is reduced. Many therapists emphasize ego functioning, attempting to strengthen the ego's ability to mediate between id and superego forces. Focusing on the ego generally involves current behavior, with less emphasis on the past.

One of the issues in psychoanalytic theories that postulate development through stages is *cultural variations in development*. Research shows that there are great differences in the way people are reared, the way they are socialized, and the kinds of problems that characterize people in different societies (Goleman, 1989). This suggests that personality development must be understood within its cultural context, rather than being seen as an invariant process based in set developmental stages. This is, of course, what we would expect from our effort in this book to integrate biological, psychological, social-structural, and cultural functioning.

Another concern with the psychoanalytic approach is its gender bias, noted by Gilligan (1982, 1990), Chodorow (1989), Chafetz (1988), and others. Freud and Erikson's developmental models consider the male experience to be the norm. By implication, if not by definition, variations are considered deviant. Psychological characteristics such as emotionalism, dependence, and passivity, for instance, have been attributed to women and interpreted as manifestations of psychopathology (Valentich, 1986:571). However, Gilligan suggests the young girl's relationship with her mother in infancy and early childhood establishes the base for her adult identity rooted in nurturance, care, and responsibility. Men, on the other hand, having separated from their mothers during their early developmental stages, define themselves in adulthood in terms of abstract qualities like justice, rather than through interpersonal relationships (Gilligan, 1982:160–161). Thus, while men and women develop different psychological characteristics, neither is better than the other. They simply stem from different life experiences and life needs. Gilligan's theories will be discussed further in Chapter 4.

Chodorow (1989), a sociologist, also challenges traditional psychoanalytic theory for its treatment of women as defective and inferior. Chodorow, like Gilligan, believes the mother-daughter relationship is the prototype of the adult capacity to relate in a caring way to others. Males, having to separate from the opposite-sex parent in order to establish their identity, often experience difficulty in maintaining intimate relations in adult life. Social learning theories stressing the role of socialization in gender identity and gender roles are more congruent with feminist thought than are traditional psychoanalytic theories (Valentich, 1986:571).

Humanistic Theories of Personality. Humanistic approaches to understanding behavior view the human person as co-creator of one's own personhood. Directed by an innate need for self-actualization, the person engages with and acts upon the environment in a mutually fulfilling way. Humanistic theories differ significantly from behavioral and psychoanalytic explanations of human behavior, but are quite compatible with cognitive theories. Both emphasize the role of will and choice in human action and underline the importance the individual assigns to the meaning of events and experiences.

Humanistic perspectives on behavior are rooted in philosophical constructs and are illuminated as much through literature and the arts as through the social and behavioral sciences. The assumptions regarding the dignity and worth of the human person and the individual's direction toward growth, inherent in these approaches, are not only congruent with social work values but could be seen as their embodiment. Humanists often find stage theories of development too linear and simplistic to explain human behavior in all its complexity. Theologians (Bianchi, 1986) warn of the dangers of turning what was intended to be descriptive into the prescriptive or normative.

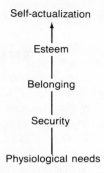

Figure 2. Maslow's Hierarchy of Needs

Abraham Maslow's need theory of human behavior is based on humanistic principles. He sees needs as able to be organized into a hierarchy, with the lower needs having to be fulfilled before higher needs can be met. Figure 2 illustrates the needs that Maslow feels are essential to full human development.

According to Maslow, physiological needs must first be met before security needs can be addressed. Needs for belonging and esteem follow, and at the apex of the hierarchy are self-actualization needs. The self-actualized human closely resembles the person who has successfully resolved Erikson's last developmental stage. Maslow's framework of human needs has obvious implications for practitioners. Lack of resources like food, clothing, and shelter leaves basic physiological needs unmet and creates almost insurmountable obstacles to meeting other kinds of needs. Difficulties in providing services to homeless families and individuals supports Maslow's assertion that basic physiological needs must be met before people can find the energy to meet their other needs.

Basic Social-Structural Concepts

Social structure, or *social organization*, refers to the ways in which social behavior becomes patterned and predictable. Underlying the concept of social structure is the belief that social behavior is, for the most part, organized and nonrandom. Several kinds of patterning occur. **Social institutions** organize activities around particular social purposes or functions, and are especially important parts of the social structure. For example, the family (a social institution) organizes categories of people—father, husbands, wives, sons, daughters, cousins, mothers-in-law, and so forth—around the performance of functions essential to the survival of society. Reproduction, socialization and care for the young, education, primary group relationships, and decision making about economic resources are examples of these important functions. Other social institutions include education, religion, politics, economics, and social welfare. Each of these organizes the behavior of large numbers of people around social functions, and thus serves to introduce order and predictability to social relationships.

Role refers to the expected behavior of categories of people within social institutions: the role of mothers, sons, and so on. Most people participate in many social institutions and occupy many roles at the same time. While the concept of role explains the predictability of much social behavior, occupying multiple roles simultaneously (mother, executive, wife) often produces **role conflict,** wherein the effective performance of one role may be in direct conflict with the effective performance of other roles. Another problem is **role strain,** when the behavioral expectations associated with a specific role are inconsistent. An example is when parents are expected to provide nurturing and discipline, yet experience these activities as somewhat incompatible.

The functions, or purposes, of social institutions are often partly **manifest functions,** which are publicly stated and assumed to be for the good of society as a whole, and partly **latent functions,** which are less publicly visible and more beneficial for some groups in society than for others. For example, the manifest function of social welfare as a social institution is to provide basic resources for those who lack them. However, the point is often made that the latent function is to control people, especially minority groups and the poor, by manipulating the resources they receive and the ways they are made available. In part, this relates to the nature of interaction among people and groups in a social structure. **Cooperative interaction** maximizes the focus on the good of group members, whereas **competitive interaction** encourages people to focus on their own good. **Conflict** can carry competition into the realm of actively destructive behavior by one group toward others.

Social structures rarely treat everyone equally. Usually there is some type of social differentiation in which criteria are used to distinguish between groups of people. Commonly used criteria are age, sex, race, ethnicity, and physical characteristics such as size, looks, and the presence of physical deficits. While such differentiation can be used simply to relate ability to activity, it may also be used to stratify people. For example, children are not allowed to drive automobiles because they lack the ability to do so, but black people may be denied housing in certain neighborhoods simply because of their skin color. **Social stratification** creates a hierarchy, a vertical arrangement of people on the basis of their access to resources or their possession of certain characteristics.

In a stratification system, some people are considered more important than others. This lays the foundation for discrimination and prejudice. **Discrimination** involves acts that disadvantage people who are considered less worthy. They are based on **prejudice,** beliefs that attribute negative characteristics to people without any concrete evidence to support those beliefs. An example of discrimination would be sending minority-group children to low-quality segregated schools because of prejudice about the intelligence of all members of minority groups.

Those with access to resources usually have power. **Power** is the ability of a person or group to enforce its will on others and it may be based on **authority,** which is legitimate power, or **coercion,** the use of illegitimate force. The importance of power is the control it provides over necessary or desirable resources—food, shelter, reputation, land, weapons, money, and so on. Those in power control the decision making that establishes the policies that determine the production and distribution of many socially desirable resources.

Most resources needed for survival and personal development are produced through the economic institution. Its social functions are to extract natural resources from the environment, produce goods from them, distribute these goods, and provide needed services. These functions are performed through the use of land, labor, capital, entrepreneurship, and technology, and those with power have more control over these economic resources. This gives them access to more goods and services, as well as the decision-making ability that enables them to protect their privileged position. As a result, inequalities between groups develop based on the amount of power they have.

In the United States, access to money is the single most important factor in ensuring access to basic life-sustaining resources. The poor have little money and thus limited ability to get the resources they need. Limited life-sustaining resources may threaten life itself, or reduce the quality of life. That is why poor people experience higher rates of disease, death, crime, social isolation, unemployment, and low levels of schooling. Thus, **poverty** can be defined as the chronic lack of adequate life-sustaining and life-enriching resources. **Social class** is the category in which the stratification process places people according to their access to life-sustaining and life-enriching resources. Those in higher social classes have more access to these resources, and those in lower social classes have less.

To understand poverty and social class, two factors are especially important. One is the very nature of economic processes. When problems occur in the relationships among the use of land, labor, capital, entrepreneurship, and technology, large-scale economic problems are likely to result. That is what happens during recessions and depressions, affecting people at all social-class levels although the poor are generally affected first and most severely.

The second factor is **social differentiation,** categorizing people on the basis of a socially defined criterion such as income, race, level of education, age, gender, sexual orientation, and so on. When social differentiation is tied to social stratification, a situation is created in which power is used by some groups (the majority groups) to maintain their own privilege (access to resources) at the expense of other groups (the minority groups). In the United States, majority groups include males, those of Western European backgrounds, Caucasians, the rich, and heterosexuals, whereas women, other racial and ethnic groups, the poor, the elderly, those with physical handicaps, and homosexuals are minorities. Membership in a minority group increases the likelihood that one's resources will be limited. For example, women and blacks are discriminated against when seeking high-paying and prestigious jobs. Affirmative action policies attempt to address these disparities in the opportunity structures.

We can see, then, that there is a clear relationship among social differentiation, social stratification, power, and access to socially desirable resources. Working effectively with people requires the ability to comprehend how these forces operate together to shape the context of human behavior. Concepts and principles learned in the disciplines of sociology, economics, and political science have direct utility for understanding these forces and for helping practitioners plan interventions that will effectively alter them.

People who occupy positions of power are concerned with preserving the existing social structure because they benefit most from it. Those who have limited access to social resources seek changes that will increase their opportunities to gain power. Hence, social-control mechanisms are often used by those in power to maintain order, and members of minority groups often perceive them as repressive. Social-control mechanisms include socialization (teaching people only socially acceptable ways to behave), **social sanctions** (socially defined positive or negative responses to behavior), and physical force, such as is vested in the criminal justice system.

Social structures organize individual behavior through groups. A **group** is two or more people who have a sense of common purpose and who interact on a regular basis. There are many kinds of groups and many specific aspects of group structure that affect the behavior of group members (decision making, leadership, group purpose, and so forth). Of particular significance is whether a group is primary or secondary. A **primary group** is generally small and is characterized by intensive, face-to-face interaction. Primary groups may be goal directed at times, but they are also structures for meeting the basic needs of their members for acceptance and personal care. **Secondary groups** are larger and generally more impersonal, and focused more on goal attainment than on meeting members' basic needs. Especially important secondary groups are **formal organizations,** such as bureaucracies. They are group structures that have clearly identified goals, as well as specified means for attaining them. They also have a hierarchical structure of relationships and an emphasis on jobs or positions rather than the specific people who perform the jobs at any particular time. Lastly, there is the expectation that interaction among members will concern job performance rather than personal desires or needs.

Formal organizations dominate industrial societies like the United States. Indeed, most social-welfare services are provided through such structures. Therefore, it is important for practitioners and anyone else seeking to help to learn how to function effectively in formal organizations. The demands can be severe, because the emphasis is on job performance rather than meeting personal needs for acceptance, creative outlets, freedom of choice, and so on. In addition, formal organizations sometimes operate slowly and with considerable organizational rigidity and complexity. Primary groups are important antidotes to the strains of large-scale secondary groups like formal organizations because primary groups do allow the expression of personal needs.

Social structure, then, determines how resources will be made available, and to whom. Groups mediate between the individual and the social structure as a whole. Looking back to earlier sections, we can see how biology generates potential that is developed through psychological means and enriched or restricted in an environment that is managed by the social structure. Nurturing environments encourage psychological growth and development consistent with biological potentials. Political climates support or inhibit the development of social structures that form the context for human behavior. Family, schools, religious institutions, and economic structures all have supporting or inhibiting effects on our actions. Social work intervention at both the micro and macro levels requires an accurate and thorough evaluation of the forces that influence human behavior.

The case material on homelessness at the end of the chapter, "Helping and Hating the Homeless" (Marin, 1987) illustrates the importance of socio-structural factors on human behavior. From the perspective of the journalist, the author points out how cultural, psychological, social-structural, and to some degree biological factors interact. The issues of physical and mental health and hunger are closely intertwined. Joe Blau (1988), also writing on the nature of homelessness, observes:

> In each historical period, people have made of homelessness what they needed to make of homelessness. In the most tolerant periods, people have admired the homeless from afar for their freedom from the demands of daily life. Even in periods of confidence, however, the existence of the disaffiliated has given rise to apprehension. This apprehension can turn harsh. When it does the Social Darwinist strain in American culture reemerges, and many blame the homeless for their own predicament. The role of progressive human service workers is to combat this view. Without denying the role of psychological factors, there is an economic and political context to which we can attest and that context must be given its due. (p. 21)

Basic Cultural Concepts

As we said earlier, culture is the repository of the commonly held values, knowledge, and material objects of a particular group or society. These aspects of a culture represent a society's way of life and are handed down to each successive generation. Culture is an end product. It evolves out of the interactions of the members of a group with one another and with their social and physical environment. As these interactions are influenced by new events, modifications are made to accommodate them.

Culture is composed of several elements. *Symbols* exist as a type of cultural shorthand. The use of symbols to represent something else requires abstract thinking because a cognitive leap from the concrete to the abstract is necessary. Numbers and language are examples of symbols. Symbols, including language, tell us much about a people. Take, for example, the recent furor in the United States regarding the burning of the American flag. The flag, to those who burned it, represented an oppressive society. To those seeking a constitutional amendment prohibiting its desecration, it clearly represents other concepts deeply embedded in our national persona: freedom and justice.

Language is an important reflection of the society in which it is found. It is through language that society most concretely and directly expresses its ideals, norms, and values. Language mirrors the experience of a society. Societies whose survival depends solely on hunting, fishing, and gathering skills may have hundreds of commonly used words to describe these activities. Their number systems may also be more basic than ours owing to the limited need for calculating large numbers. A postindustrial society whose members buy their food in grocery stores will have radically different language and numerical systems. Consider, for example, how common are words related to computer technology: user-friendly, megabytes, printout, feedback, loops, and so on.

Language not only reflects but also influences culture. Take, for example, the commonly used term "primitive" to describe certain non-Western societies or the action of members of groups within our own society. The word "primitive" to many denotes not only undeveloped but also inferior. The use of such language promotes continued ethnocentric thinking.

Values are transmitted through symbols and language. **Values** are commonly held beliefs of a society's members. Think of some of the cliches used in the early and middle part of this century that reflected society's view of women: "A woman's place is in the home" or "women are too emotional to be decision makers." While these cliches reflect values that are still widely held, they are beginning to lose some of their potency. Topics such as free enterprise, school prayer, abortion, affirmative action, and funding for "star wars" all reflect values. These values are sometimes shared by a large number of people, sometimes by only a few. Often they are in conflict. As a nation we appear to be in conflict over our appreciation of nature and our demand for natural resources, for example. As stated in Chapter 1 in reference to a priori knowledge, symbols and myths are embedded in personal and cultural experiences. They are also found to reflect spirituality (generic) and religion (specific structures and rituals). As such they contain and transmit specific values in service of social integration.

Values influence behavior by acting as guideposts that tell the person which beliefs and corresponding actions will be positively sanctioned (rewarded) or negatively sanctioned (punished). Sanctions are reflected in a society's **norms,** which are the specific rules to govern behavior that are based on social values.

Society dictates that one does not cut into a line of moviegoers waiting to purchase a ticket. It is considered normative for a widow or widower to observe certain mourning rituals for a given period of time. Behaviors that violate norms are sanctioned formally through laws or informally in subtle but effective ways. While a person who attends a formal dinner wearing sport clothes may not face arrest, that individual may not be invited again.

It is clear that variations exist within a culture in the way people think and act. This is due to **subcultures,** smaller groups existing within the large group that have some unique cultural characteristics. Italian-Americans, for example, have different values and behaviors with respect to the family from those of Native Americans. It is important to remember, however, that even within subcultures there is a great deal of intragroup variation. It is unsafe to assume that any individual member of a group will behave in ways consistent with the predominant patterns attributed to the subculture with which he or she identifies. To assume that because someone is a first-generation migrant from Appalachia she or he will behave in a predictable fashion may well be incorrect because it is based on a stereotype. Members of cultural groups generally share certain beliefs, values, and behaviors, but each individual combines these in unique ways that reflect his or her particular situation.

Subcultures usually coexist in such a way as to preserve the structure of the larger culture of which they are a part. This harmonious coexistence of different subcultural groups is called **cultural pluralism.** It recognizes the legitimacy of the traditions of diverse subcultures. Cultural diversity is seen as a resource to be encouraged when viewed from the perspective of cultural pluralism. As a pattern of racial and ethnic relations, cultural pluralism is in contrast to the melting-pot philosophy that traditionally characterized American society. The melting-pot approach sought to fuse all diverse racial and ethnic subcultures into one ''American blend.'' Cultural pluralism is more accepting of the value of different cultural groups and recognizes the need to preserve as well as blend them.

Ethnocentrism refers to cultures or subcultures evaluating each other on the basis of their own cultural elements. Ethnocentric thinking usually leads to one culture denigrating another, since each culture believes its own way of doing things is the best way. Practitioners have to remember that the cultural integrity of each group is the only appropriate context for understanding its behavior. Just because some elements of a subculture may create difficulties for its members as they function in the larger culture does not mean that either group is right or wrong. Careful negotiation based on mutual respect is required to see that the needs of both groups are met in ways appropriate to each.

Behavior that violates a group's norms is considered **deviant.** Behavior can only be judged acceptable or unacceptable when it is evaluated according to some standard—the norm which is based on cultural values. When groups have different standards based in cultural differences, they may have difficulty accepting each other's behavior. For example, the management of time is one of the factors that varies among cultures and subcultures. This sometimes leads members of one group to accuse members of other groups of being deviant by being late for appointments or unconcerned about "efficiency." This is an example of ethnocentrism, since the majority group is using its standards to judge the behavior of other groups. Obviously there is nothing inherently right or wrong about any group's management of time. It is only right or wrong with respect to some standard, and different cultural or subcultural groups often have different norms regarding time.

Attempts to apply universal standards of behavior to all situations are the result of ethnocentric thinking patterns. Power becomes a relevant factor in these situations, because the majority group may attempt to impose its standards on others. The majority group often justifies doing so by making reference to its own cultural or subcultural values, an example of how ethnocentrism can be used to denigrate other cultures. Practitioners need to be constantly vigilant so as to avoid this type of behavior.

As we can see, culture is a powerful influence on behavior because it serves to organize a society's social structure, which in turn governs people's actions. Once again we return to the continuum from biological through cultural behavior. Figure 3 demonstrates the interacting nature of the four sources of behavior—the biological, psychological, social-structural, and cultural. Kimmel (1980) conceptualizes the dynamic interaction between the individual and society on a private-public continuum. The private (darkly shaded) area of Figure 3 represents those aspects of personality that are internal and inaccessible to others. Included in the public sources of behavior are cultural beliefs, social norms, and social institutions. Change introduced in either the private or public areas affects the other.

Although we have analyzed behavior in terms of its four sources, sooner or later we must combine them to create a sense of person-in-environment interaction. Each concept discussed in this chapter helps us understand some part of this interactive whole, and each deserves careful study. But understanding how they all interact to become useful and practical tools for attaining the purposes of the helping professions is our ultimate goal. The next chapter will focus on this goal, showing how all of these concepts can be integrated so that practice is supported by a holistic view of human behavior.

SUMMARY

This chapter has presented an overview of the biological, psychological, social-structural, and cultural dimensions of human behavior. Selected concepts from

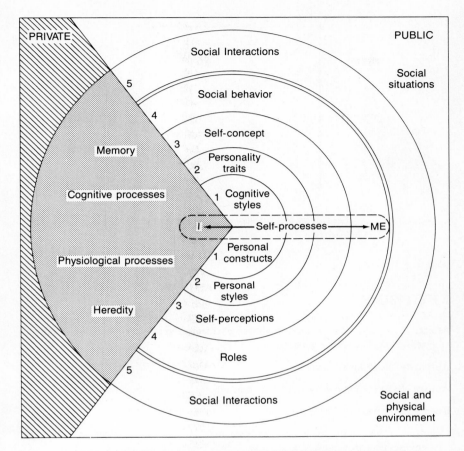

Figure 3. The Holistic Quality of Human Behavior (*Adulthood and Aging: An Interdisciplinary Development View,* Doug Kimmel. Copyright © 1980 John Wiley & Sons, Inc. Reprinted by permission of John Wiley & Sons, Inc.)

the biological, social, and behavioral sciences that are useful to the social welfare professional have been reviewed. The goal of professional social work practice is improving the transactions between people and their environments. Knowledge geared toward understanding the factors influencing these transactions comes from several disciplines and demands of the practitioner the ability to select, integrate, and apply information from diverse sources. The following chapter will provide a framework that will help the professional pull together selected concepts in a way that is useful in developing a holistic viewpoint regarding human behavior.

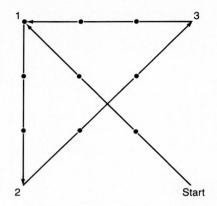

Solution to the nine-dot configuration on p. 38.

KEY TERMS

Affect. The feelings and emotions that become attached to information derived from our sensory and cognitive processes.

Authority. Legitimate power.

Autism. Severe emotional withdrawal from others.

Coercion. The use of illegitimate force.

Cognition. The ability to process and organize information in order to utilize the environment to achieve one's goals.

Competitive interaction. Interaction that encourages people to focus on their own good.

Conflict. Actively destructive behavior by one group toward others.

Cooperative interaction. Interaction that focuses on the good of group members.

Cultural pluralism. The harmonious coexistence of different subcultural groups.

Culture. The values, knowledge, and material technology that people learn to accept as appropriate and desirable, and that are passed down from generation to generation.

Death. The point at which the human body is no longer able to sustain itself.

Degenerative processes. The genetically determined deterioration of cells as the human body ages at a rate and in a pattern unique to each person.

Deviance. Behavior that violates a group's norm.

Discrimination. Acts that disadvantage those who are considered less worthy.

Ethnocentrism. When cultures or subcultures evaluate each other on the basis of their own cultural elements.

Explanatory knowledge. Knowledge that seeks only to explain phenomenon, not to change or alter it.

Formal organization. Hierarchical secondary group structures that have clearly identified goals, as well as specified means for attaining them.

Genetic engineering. Purposeful modification of genetic material in the laboratory.

Group. Two or more people who have a sense of common purpose and interact on a regular basis.

Homeostasis. Maintenance of a relatively steady state of a system.

Intervention knowledge. Knowledge that is usable to influence or change human behavior.

Latent functions of social institutions. Functions that are less publicly visible and more beneficial for some groups in society than for others.

Life. A physiological process that entails the management of complex chemical processes mediated by the brain through an elaborate series of neurological impulses.

Life span. The period from conception to death.

Manifest functions of social institutions. Functions that are publicly stated and assumed to be for the good of society as a whole.

Mutation. A process in which genes are changed from their original form.

Norms. Specific rules that govern behavior and that are based on social values.

Nurturance. The protection and caring needed for psychological well-being.

Nutrition. Basic nutrients needed for physical health.

Pain. A warning that some part of the physical system is being pushed toward its adaptive limit.

Perception. The ability to see, smell, feel, and touch, and to develop organized responses to the sensory characteristics of the environment.

Personality. The integrating psychological structure that develops to help the individual function in the environment.

Physiological health. When the genetic plan is able to unfold because the resources needed to permit growth and development have been provided.

Poverty. Chronic lack of adequate life-sustaining and life-enriching resources.

Power. Ability of a person or group to enforce its will on others.

Prejudice. Beliefs that attribute negative characteristics to people without any concrete evidence to support those beliefs.

Primary group. Generally small groups that are characterized by intensive face-to-face interaction.

Reflex. Genetically programmed predisposition to act.

Role. The expected behavior of categories of people within social institutions.

Role conflict. When the effective performance of one role may be in direct conflict with the effective performance of others.

Role strain. When the behavioral expectations associated with a specific role are inconsistent.

Secondary groups. Groups that are generally large and impersonal, focused more on goal attainment than on meeting members' basic needs.

Social class. The category in which the stratification process places people according to their access to life-sustaining and life-enriching resources.

Social differentiation. Categorizing people on the basis of a socially defined criterion.

Social institutions. Social structures that organize activities around particular social purposes or function, such as the family and religion.

Social sanctions. Socially defined positive or negative responses to behavior.

Social stratification. A vertical ranking of people on the basis of their access to resources or their possession of certain characteristics.

Social structure. Socially created structures, such as the family, the church, schools, and the economic system, that exist to organize and pattern social interaction.

Socialization. The process through which people acquire the beliefs, customs, values, and attitudes of their culture.

Subculture. A small group existing within a larger cultural group that has some unique cultural characteristics.

Values. Commonly held beliefs of a society's members.

STUDY QUESTIONS

1. Compare and contrast biological, psychological, social-structural, and cultural perspectives on homelessness, using the article "Helping and Hating the Homeless" in Exhibit 1. Which do you think is most helpful in understanding homelessness? Why?
2. Using the same article, explain how these same four sources of behavior help you as a social work practitioner to understand the multidimensional nature of homelessness.

3. About which of the four sources of behavior do you feel most knowledgeable? Why do you know more about some than about others? Does this tell you something about cultural values, education as a social institution, and your own interests and experiences? How committed are you to expanding your knowledge in those areas in which you are presently less knowledgeable? How might you do so?

4. When are you most likely to consciously assess your resources? Have you ever thought of them as including biological, psychological, social-structural, and cultural components? Thinking of them in this way, do you consider that you have more or fewer resources than you have previously thought? How about obstacles—do you see more or less of these in your life using the framework presented in this chapter?

5. Thinking about obstacles (biological, psychological, social-structural, and cultural), what group in society do you think is most affected by each of the four types of obstacles (for example, the elderly having especially severe biological obstacles)? Explain what these obstacles are and why you consider them especially important in terms of their effects on the lives of the people involved. Do you think others would agree with your selection of the groups with the most severe obstacles? Why or why not? Finally, can you also identify resources each group might use in coping with the obstacles you have identified?

6. Traditional psychoanalytic theories have been challenged for their gender bias. Why are social learning theories of human behavior more congruent with feminist thought than with psychoanalytical theories?

REFERENCES

Auden, W. H. (1986). In E. Mendelson, ed., *The English Auden: Poems, Essays and Dramatic Writings 1927–1939*. Towbridge, Great Britain: Redwood Burn, Ltd., p. 342.

Bandura, A. (1977). *Social Learning Theory*. Englewood Cliffs, NJ: Prentice-Hall.

Bianchi, E. (1986). *Aging as a Spiritual Journey*. New York: Crossroad Publishing.

Blau, J. (1988). On the Uses of Homelessness: A Literature Review. *Catalyst*, Vol. 6, No. 21.

Bower, B. (1989). Growing up Sad: Depression in Children Attracts Scrutiny. *Science News*, Vol. 136, No. 6 (August 5), pp. 90–91.

Brody, J. (1981). Effects of Beauty Found to Run Surprisingly Deep. *New York Times*, September 1, pp. C1ff.

Campbell, J. (1988). *The Power of Myth*. New York: Doubleday.

Carlson, M. (1988). *Meaning-Making: Therapeutic Processes in Adult Development*. New York: W. W. Norton.

Chafetz, J. (1988). *Feminist Sociology: An Overview of Contemporary Theories*. Itasca, IL: F. E. Peacock Publishers.

Chodorow, N. (1989). *Feminism and Psychoanalysis*. New Haven, CT: Yale University Press.

Craig, G. (1986). *Human Development*, 4th ed. Englewood Cliffs, NJ: Prentice-Hall.

Erikson, E. (1976). *Adulthood.* New York: W. W. Norton.

Gambrill, E. (1987). Behavioral Approach. In *Encyclopedia of Social Work,* 18th ed. Silver Spring, MD: National Association of Social Workers, pp. 184–194.

Gans, H. (1971). The Uses of Poverty: The Poor Pay All. *Social Policy,* July–August, pp. 20–24.

Gilligan, C. (1982). *In a Different Voice: Psychological Theory and Women's Development.* Cambridge, MA: Harvard University Press.

Gilligan, C., ed. (1990). *Making Connections: The Relational World of Adolescent Girls at Emma Willard School.* Cambridge, MA: Harvard University Press.

Goleman, D. (1986). Major Personality Study Finds That Traits Are Mostly Inherited. *New York Times,* December 2, pp. C1ff.

———— (1987). Personality: Major Traits Found Stable Through Life. *New York Times,* June 9, pp. C1ff.

———— (1988). Erikson, in His Own Old Age, Expands His View of Life. *New York Times,* June 14, pp. C1ff.

———— (1989). From Tokyo to Tampa, Different Ideas of Self. *New York Times,* March 7, pp. 17ff.

Kimmel, D. C. (1980). *Adulthood and Aging: An Interdisciplinary Development View.* New York: Wiley, pp. 398–401.

Langer, J. (1969). *Theories of Development.* New York: Holt, Rinehart & Winston, pp. 51–73, 107–156.

Leavitt, D. (1989). The Way I Live Now. *New York Times Magazine,* July 9, pp. 28ff.

Lozoff, B. (1989). Nutrition and Behavior. *American Psychologist,* Vol. 44, No. 2, pp. 231–236.

Marin, P. (1987). Helping and Hating the Homeless: The Struggle at the Margins of America. *Harper's,* January, pp. 39ff.

Miller, H. (1970). The Relevance of the Humanities. *American Scholar,* Winter, p. 105.

Newberger, C. M. and E. DeVos (1988). Abuse and Victimization: A Life-Span Developmental Perspective. *American Journal of Orthopsychiatry,* Vol. 58, No. 4 (October), pp. 505–511.

Plomin, R. (1989). Environment and Genes. *American Psychologist,* Vol. 44, No. 2, pp. 105–111.

Reich, T. and others. (1987). The Familial Transmission of Primary Major Depressive Disorder. *Journal of Psychiatric Research,* Vol. 21, pp. 613–624.

Schmeck, Jr., H. (1987). Burst of Discoveries Reveals Genetic Basis for Many Diseases. *New York Times,* March 31, pp. C1ff.

Science News (1989). Modifying Mendel One More Time. Vol. 136, No. 6 (August 5), p. 92.

Seltzer, M. (1989). Random and Not So Random Thoughts on Becoming a Statistic: Professional and Personal Musings. *International Journal of Aging and Human Development,* Vol. 28, No. 1, pp. 4–5.

Shakespeare, W. (1947). *Hamlet,* act 1, scene 5, lines 165–166 in *Yale Shakespeare,* J. R. Crawford, ed. New Haven, CT: Yale University Press.

Sherman, E. (1987). Cognitive Therapy. In *Encyclopedia of Social Work*, 18th ed. Silver Spring, MD: National Association of Social Workers, pp. 288–291.

Snyderman, M. and S. Rothman (1987). Survey and Expert Opinions on Intelligence and Aptitude Testing. *American Psychologist,* Vol. 42, pp. 137–144.

Thompson, W. R. (1968). Genetics and Personality. In E. Norbeck and others, eds., *The Study of Personality*. New York: Holt, Rinehart & Winston, pp. 161–174.

Valentich, M. (1986). Feminism and Social Work Practice. In F. Turner, ed., *Social Work Treatment: Interlocking Theoretical Approaches*, 3rd ed. New York: Free Press, pp. 564–589.

Wallace, J. (1989). A Biopsychosocial Model of Alcoholism. *Social Casework*, Vol. 70, No. 6, pp. 325–332.

Watzlawick, K. P., J. Weakland and R. Fisch. (1974). *Change: Principles of Problem Formation and Problem Resolution*. New York: W. W. Norton.

EXHIBIT 1   HELPING AND HATING THE HOMELESS

The following excerpts are from Peter Marin, "Helping and Hating the Homeless,"
Harper's *magazine, January 1987, pp. 39ff. In this article the author describes the*
homeless, the reality of their lives, and the complexities in solving the homeless
problem. His analysis illustrates the systemic nature of human behavior and the
human diversity inherent in any kind of social activity.

The trouble begins with the word "homeless." It has become such an abstraction,
and is applied to so many different kinds of people, with so many different histories
and problems, that it is almost meaningless.

Homelessness, in itself, is nothing more than a condition visited upon men and
women (and, increasingly, children) as the final stage of a variety of problems about
which the word "homelessness" tells us almost nothing. Or, to put it another way, it
is a catch basin into which pour all of the people disenfranchised or marginalized or
scared off by processes beyond their control, those which lie close to the heart of
American life. Here are the groups packed into the single category of "the homeless."

- Veterans, mainly from the war in Vietnam. In many American cities, vets make up
  close to 50 percent of all homeless males.
- The mentally ill. In some parts of the country, roughly a quarter of the homeless
  would, a couple of decades ago, have been institutionalized.
- The physically disabled or chronically ill, who do not receive any benefits or
  whose benefits do not enable them to afford permanent shelter.
- The elderly on fixed incomes whose funds are no longer sufficient for their needs.
- Men, women, and whole families pauperized by the loss of a job.
- Single parents, usually women, without the resources or skills to establish new
  lives.
- Runaway children, many of whom have been abused.
- Alcoholics and those in trouble with drugs (whose troubles often begin with one of
  the other conditions listed here).
- Immigrants, both legal and illegal, who often are not counted among the homeless
  because they constitute a "problem" in their own right.
- Traditional tramps, hobos, and transients, who have taken to the road or the streets
  for a variety of reasons and who prefer to be there.

You can quickly learn two things abut the homeless from this list. First, you can
learn that many of the homeless, before they were homeless, were people more or
less like ourselves: members of the working or middle class. And you can learn that
the world of the homeless has its roots in various policies, events, and ways of life
for which some of us are responsible and from which some of us actually prosper.

We decide, as a people, to go to war, we ask our children to kill and to die, and
the result, years later, is grown men homeless on the street.

We change, with the best intentions, the laws pertaining to the mentally ill, and then, without intention, neglect to provide them with services; and the result, in our streets, drives some of us crazy with rage.

We cut taxes and prune budgets, we modernize industry and shift the balance of trade, and the result of all these actions and errors can be read, sleeping form by sleeping form, on our city streets.

The liberals cannot blame the conservatives. The conservatives cannot blame the liberals. Homelessness is the *sum total* of our dreams, policies, intentions, errors, omissions, cruelties, kindnesses, all of it recorded, in flesh, in the life of the streets.

You can also learn from this list one of the most important things there is to know about the homeless—that they can be roughly divided into two groups: those who have had homelessness forced upon them and want nothing more than to escape it; and those who have at least in part *chosen* it for themselves. . . .

The fact is, many of the homeless are not only hapless victims but voluntary exiles . . . , people who have turned not against life itself but against *us,* our life, American life. Look for a moment at the vets. The price of returning to America was to forget what they had seen or learned in Vietnam, to ''put it behind them.'' But some could not do that, and the stress of trying showed up as alcoholism, broken marriages, drug addiction, crime. And it showed up too as life on the street, which was for some vets a desperate choice made in the name of life—the best they could manage. It was a way of avoiding what might have occurred had they stayed where they were: suicide, or violence done to others.

We must learn to accept that there may indeed be people, and not only vets, who have seen so much of our world, or seen it so clearly, that to live in it becomes impossible. . . .

It is important to . . . recognize the immensity of the changes that have occurred in the marginal world in the past twenty years. . . .

There began to pour into the marginal world—slowly in the sixties, a bit faster in the seventies, and then faster still in the eighties—more and more people who neither belonged nor knew how to survive there. The sixties brought the counterculture and drugs; the streets filled with young dropouts. Changes in the law loosed upon the streets mentally ill men and women. Inflation took its toll, then recession. Working-class and even middle-class men and women—entire families—began to fall into a world they did not understand.

As the same time the transient world was being inundated by new inhabitants, its landscape, its economy, was shrinking radically. Jobs became harder to find. Modernization had something to do with it: machines took the place of men and women. And the influx of workers from Mexico and points farther south created a class of semipermanent workers who took the place of casual transient labor. More important, perhaps, was the fact that the forgotten parts of many cities began to attract attention. Downtown areas were redeveloped, reclaimed. The skid-row sections of smaller cities were turned into ''old townes.'' The old hotels that once catered to transients were upgraded or torn down or became warehouses for welfare families—an arrangement far more profitable to the owners. The price of housing increased: evictions increased. The mentally ill, who once could afford to house themselves in cheap rooms, the alcoholics, who once would drink themselves to sleep at night in their cheap hotels, were out on the street—exposed to the weather and to danger, and also in plain and public view: "problems" to be dealt with. . . .

The homeless, simply because they are homeless, are strangers, alien—and therefore a threat. Their presence, in itself, comes to constitute a kind of violence; it deprives us of our sense of safety. . . .

What I am getting at here is the *nature* of the desire to help the homeless—what is hidden behind it and why it so often does harm. Every government program, almost every private project, is geared as much to the needs of those giving help as it is to the needs of the homeless. Go to any government agency, or, for that matter, to most private charities, and you will find yourself enmeshed, at once, in a bureaucracy so tangled and oppressive, or confronted with so much moral arrogance and contempt, that you will be driven back out into the streets for relief. . . .

It is these attitudes, in various forms and permutations, that you find repeated endlessly in America. We are moved either to "redeem" the homeless or to punish them. Perhaps there is nothing consciously hostile about it. Perhaps it is simply that as the machinery of bureaucracy cranks itself up to deal with these problems, attitudes assert themselves automatically. But whatever the case, the fact remains that almost every one of our strategies for helping the homeless is simply an attempt to rearrange the world *cosmetically,* in terms of how it looks and smells to *us.* Compassion is little more than the passion for control.

The central question emerging from all this is, What does a society owe to its members in trouble, and *how* is that debt to be paid? It is a question which must be answered in two parts; first, in relation to the men and women who have been marginalized against their will, and then, in a slightly different way, in relation to those who have chosen (or accept or even prize) their marginality.

As for those who have been marginalized against their wills, I think the general answer is obvious: A society owes its members whatever it takes for them to regain their places in the social order. And when it comes to specific remedies, one need only read backward the various processes which have created homelessness and then figure out where help is likely to do the most good. But the real point here is not the specific remedies required—affordable housing, say—but the basis upon which they must be offered, the necessary underlying ethical notion we seem in this nation unable to grasp: that those who are the inevitable casualties of modern industrial capitalism and the free-market system are entitled, *by right,* and by the simple virtue of their participation in that system, to whatever help they need. They are entitled to help to find and hold their places in the society whose social contract they have, in effect, signed and observed.

Look at that for just a moment: the notion of a contract. The majority of homeless Americans have kept, insofar as they could, to the terms of that contract. In any shelter these days you can find men and women who have worked ten, twenty, forty years, and whose lives have nonetheless come to nothing. There are people who cannot afford a place in the world they helped create. And in return? Is it life on the street they have earned? Or the cruel charity we so grudgingly grant them?

But those marginalized against their will are only half the problem. There remains, still, the question of whether we owe anything to those who are voluntarily marginal. What about them: the street people, the rebels, and the recalcitrants, those who have torn up their social contracts or returned them unsigned? . . .

We owe them, I think, at least a place to exist, a way to exist. That may not be a *moral* obligation, in the sense that our obligation to the involuntarily marginal is clearly a moral one, but it is an obligation nevertheless, one you might call an existential obligation. . . .

I think we as a society need men like [those who choose to live on the margins]. A society needs its margins as much as it needs art and literature. It need holes and gaps, *breathing spaces,* let us say, into which men and women can escape and live, when necessary, in ways otherwise denied them. Margins guarantee to society a flexibility, an elasticity, and allow it to accommodate itself to the natures and needs of its members. When margins vanish, society becomes too rigid, too oppressive by far, and therefore inimical to life. . . .

CHAPTER 3

The Integrating Framework

Upon this age, that never speaks its mind,
This furtive age, this age endowed with power
To wake the moon with footsteps, fit an oar
Into the rowlocks of the wind, and find
What swims before his prow, what swirls behind—
Upon this gifted age, in its dark hour,
Rains from the sky a meteoric shower
Of facts . . . they lie unquestioned, uncombined.
Wisdom enough to leech us of our ill
Is daily spun; but there exists no loom
To weave it into fabric; undefiled
Proceeds pure Science, and has her say; but still
Upon this world from the collective womb
Is spewed all day the red triumphant child.

Edna St. Vincent Millay*

CHAPTER OVERVIEW

An intake social worker in a family planning clinic interviews a 35-year-old woman and her 14-year-old pregnant daughter. The mother is crying and explaining that she has tried to raise her daughter properly but fears she has failed.

---

*"Upon this age, that never speaks its mind," by Edna St. Vincent Millay. From *Collected Sonnets*, Revised and Expanded Edition, Harper & Row, 1988. Copyright © 1939, 1967 by Edna St. Vincent Millay and Norma Millay Ellis. Reprinted by permission of Elizabeth Barnett, Literary Executor.

She is unsure how to help her daughter or how she can afford to support another child in the home.

A social worker in a community center that serves a primarily low-income Hispanic population experiences concern regarding a proposed urban renewal project that threatens existing housing in the neighborhood. The residents are becoming increasingly angry over the situation and tensions are rising.

A social worker with a multiservice agency that provides latchkey services to neighborhood children is confronted with the closing of the program because of the redirection of priorities to other programs.

A social worker assigned to a home for the elderly is informed by the Residents' Rights Council of their concern that many of the elderly are being overmedicated, and that little attention is being given to providing opportunities for residents' personal and social development.

The above examples are representative of the range of practice situations encountered by social workers. Being effective in addressing such diverse problems and needs requires an understanding of the forces, events, and processes that underlie them. Chapter 1 raised the question of what knowledge and skills are necessary for beginning generalist social work practitioners so that they can practice effectively in the diverse situations they will encounter. Chapter 2 focused on specific kinds of knowledge that social workers need. Concepts and theories from biology, psychology, sociology, and anthropology were briefly surveyed so that the biological, psychological, social-structural, and cultural dimensions of behavior can be understood. You will recall that the purpose of this review was to emphasize the holistic nature of human behavior.

In this chapter we will develop a framework that organizes the concepts and theories reviewed in the previous chapter so that they can be used in practice. The framework is a **model**, a way of organizing related concepts and theories. Its purpose in this chapter is to take related concepts and theories from the social, biological, and behavioral sciences and apply them to the human behavior that social workers encounter in their daily practice—behavior such as that described in the short anecdotes that open this chapter. Upon completing this chapter you will have more than an assortment of specific concepts and theories. You will in addition have a way to relate these concepts and theories to each other so that they can be applied in practice situations. As a result you will have a holistic perspective when viewing practice situations.

SCREENS AND FRAMEWORKS

A *screen* is a device used to separate the finer from the coarser parts of a substance, or, to use a more common expression, to separate the wheat from the chaff. Think for a minute of a screen as a kind of sieve through which ideas filter.

Some ideas are filtered out, unable to sift through the mesh. Other ideas filter through easily. The health, growth, and ecological perspectives presented in Chapter 1 can be thought of as screens through which information and data are filtered. The screen in this instance filters information by asking three questions:

1. Does the information or data focus on health, wellness, and competence, or does it emphasize pathology?
2. Does the information emphasize growth or illness?
3. Does the information consider the multiple dimensions of human behavior, or does it stress only one, such as psychological functioning?

Applying this screen to the theories of human behavior reviewed in the previous chapter, we can see how cognitive, humanistic, and social-learning theories filter through with more ease than do psychoanalytic theories, which emphasize mental illness and focus on pathology early in life. This is not to say that the theories that are filtered out are wrong. We are not attempting to filter, according to right or wrong, questions that depend on many years of research to determine. Instead, we are trying to identify through the filtering process those theories that will help us to understand the person-in-situation since that is the approach taken in social work. This is the view that is congruent with the value base of the profession, which sees supporting strengths and promoting competence as more effective than focusing on deficits (Weick and others, 1989).

The framework of this chapter also functions as a screen. It sifts information from the biological, social, and behavioral sciences (especially the disciplines of sociology, psychology, biology, and anthropology) to find the concepts, theories, and data that help us to understand how the multiple dimensions of human behavior interact. Our goal in using the framework (the sieve) is to understand human behavior in its wholeness. As we shall see, this understanding includes what people are trying to accomplish in their lives (their life goals) as well as the strategies they use in trying to attain these goals. Figure 4 diagrams how the framework functions as a screen.

Biological, psychological, social-structural, and cultural factors affecting people's identification of life goals and strategies to attain them can serve as either resources or obstacles. **Resources** are factors that facilitate people's ability to define and achieve life goals, while **obstacles** are factors that inhibit goal definition and attainment. Because humans have relatively few genetically programmed reflexes, they are heavily dependent on each other for physical care and social learning. Biological and psychological characteristics that facilitate interaction with others—physical attractiveness and an outgoing personality, for example—are likely to be resources as people attempt to identify their life goals and work toward attaining them. On the other hand, social-structural and cultural conditions that lead to alienation and conflict may impede the formation of healthy life goals and behavioral strategies. Prejudice and discrimination illus-

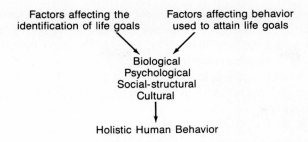

Figure 4. Identifying Elements of Holisitic Behavior

trate how these social-structural and cultural forces can operate to impede rather than facilitate healthy human behavior.

Keep in mind that the interaction of resources and obstacles is complex and subtle. Anything can be either a resource or an obstacle, depending on the way it is used and the context in which it occurs. Intelligence is usually considered a resource, yet people of high intelligence may be at a disadvantage in situations requiring the strict observance of rules and the performance of highly routinized activities. Physical limitations, such as blindness or quadraplegia, are most often thought of as obstacles, yet they can also enable people to find resources of strength, courage, and creativity that would have otherwise been ignored. The framework that you will learn in this chapter requires that you screen ideas very carefully. The interaction of biological, psychological, social-structural, and cultural factors that leads to holistic behavior must be approached with sensitivity and without stereotypes about what behavior is "good" and what is "bad." Our task as practitioners is to understand what facilitates goal definition and attainment, and also what impedes them. The framework will allow you to sift out the resources and obstacles as long as you don't impose your own biases that limit your analysis.

THE FRAMEWORK FOR INTEGRATING AND APPLYING KNOWLEDGE

There are three parts to the framework that will be developed in this chapter to help you view behavior holistically, seeing the resources and obstacles in biological, psychological, social-structural, and cultural dimensions of behavior. These three parts consist of the following:

1. *Systems.* A systems perspective aids us in our attempt to maintain a holistic view. It focuses on the whole, and how the parts of the whole interact so that outcomes are affected.

2. *Human diversity.* Human diversity helps us to see why dimensions of behavior become either resources or obstacles for people according to their characteristics, their goals, their needs, their preferred behavior patterns, and their environment.

3. *Directionality.* Directionality aids us in our search for purpose, and for order and pattern in human behavior that sometimes seems highly idiosyncratic and even illogical. These three components of the framework are illustrated in Figure 5.

To illustrate how the framework is applied, let us consider how we might try to understand and help parents who have abused their children. There are many stresses that could lead to child abuse. A parent suffering from malnutrition may lack the energy necessary to perform even minimal parenting tasks. Poverty and unemployment (social-structural factors) may create anxiety and withdrawal that impede relating to one's own children, as well as the lack of resources needed to meet children's basic needs. A parent with a rigid personality may become furious and abusive when a child becomes soiled or makes a mistake. Cultures differ in their expectations about discipline, setting the stage for one culture to consider abusive what in another culture is considered normal parental discipline.

In addition to their individual effects on child abuse, the above factors may interact. Some cultures encourage relatives or friends to take over child-care

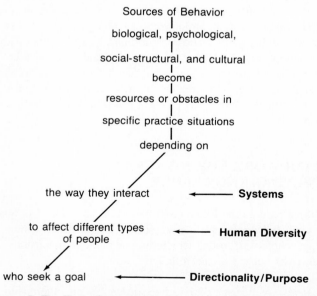

Figure 5. The Three Components of the Human Behavior Framework

functions when parents are having difficulty rearing their children, thus avoiding abuse and giving the parents opportunities to address other problems. Other cultures prefer to offer the struggling parents help through the formal social welfare system, leaving the children in the home unless conditions are extreme. Meeting biological needs, such as for adequate nutrition, may also be tied to the availability of social-structural resources like income assistance or medical care. Psychological problems that impede childrearing may themselves be the result of childhood traumas, current marital or employment difficulties, physical addiction to drugs or alcohol, or even genetic factors. Their impact on the child will be affected by available treatment resources (social-structural) as well as cultural values regarding definitions of mental illness and appropriate treatment.

You can see from this example that human behavior is indeed complex. However, notice how the major elements of the framework are illustrated. Biological, psychological, social-structural, and cultural dimensions of behavior are systematically explored to identify their impact on causing the problem and providing possible solutions. For example, malnutrition is a cause because it drains the parents' energy needed to care for children, and its solution is to help provide adequate nutrition through increased income, medical care, and so on. Each dimension is viewed as either a possible resource or an obstacle as we see when cultural values may help solve child abuse (by letting others take over childrearing for dysfunctional parents), or when they make it more difficult to solve the problem (by allowing parents to continue to use physically damaging discipline).

In addition, the systemic nature of child abuse is illustrated by seeing how parenting is affected by such factors as employment, poverty, and psychological functioning. Thus, child abuse is itself linked to other behaviors and structures. These linkages will vary for different groups. Those groups most affected by poverty, such as single-parent households headed by women or minority families, will endure more stress as a result of inadequate environmental resources. Finally, directionality (purpose) is important. When parents abuse children it is important to determine how this behavior fits into the life goals of the abusing parents. Rarely do parents purposely intend to abuse their children. In most cases, they want to be good parents but lack resources or information. This suggests intervention strategies that will help them move toward their real goal— competent parenting—rather than punishing them for failures that they themselves would like to avoid.

Table 4 shows how the framework can be used to understand practice situations holistically. The table illustrates how the four sources of behavior— biological, psychological, social-structural, and cultural—offer both resources and obstacles. These resources and obstacles may be found in the systems, human diversity, and directionality that characterize each of the four sources of behavior. The following sections provide a fuller discussion of each of the systems, human diversity, and directionality components of the framework.

TABLE 4. FRAMEWORK FOR USING KNOWLEDGE TO UNDERSTAND PRACTICE SITUATIONS HOLISTICALLY

The Role of Resources and Obstacles in Behavior

Perspectives for a Holistic View	Biological		Psychological		Social-Structural		Cultural	
	R	O	R	O	R	O	R	O
Systems								
Human diversity								
Directionality								

R = Resource; O = Obstacle

SYSTEMS

A **system** can be defined as a whole made up of mutually interdependent parts. Systems theory states that in any system a change in one part has an impact on others. We will also see that systems influence each other through the exchange of resources. The idea of systems can be readily grasped by looking at the ecology of planet Earth. Recent concern has been expressed about the so-called greenhouse effect. Briefly stated, scientists believe that the planet's temperature is rising, which threatens all life on earth: The polar ice caps will melt, raising ocean levels and shifting temperate weather zones—all of these can radically alter earth's fragile ecological balance. Rachel Carson (1987) in her book *The Silent Spring* expressed concern that the delicate balance of earth's biological life forms were in danger of being lethally altered by pollution and destruction of natural resources. The earth's life forms can be seen as a system. Cutting down rain forests in South America and Africa depletes the production of oxygen in the atmosphere and also diminishes earth's capacity to moderate its temperature, thereby affecting all life forms. Thus, we can see how one part of a system (depleting rain forests) affects other parts (depleting oxygen in the atmosphere).

A system can also be visualized as a series of smaller units nestled inside progressively larger ones. In the example of planet Earth, a city that discharges untreated sewage into a river illustrates how one system (the city) affects another system (the ecology of the river), with both being part of the larger system called planet Earth. Similar relationships can be see in human systems. Individuals, families, small groups (work, school, and friendship groups), bureaucratic organizations, communities, societies, cultures, and ultimately the community of humankind are all systems. Each affects the other as, for example, when wage decisions made in the workplace affect the income of workers' families. In addition, we can see how larger systems, like communities, are composed of smaller systems, such as families and other small groups. A systems perspective provides a model that focuses on multiple levels of phenomena simultaneously (families, the workplace, and community life, for example), and it also emphasizes the interaction between behavioral units (what happens in families is affected by what occurs in the workplace, continuing the above example). The result is that a systems view helps the social-work practitioner understand behavior in context and shows how these units of varying size and levels of complexity mutually influence each other.

It is important to remember from a systems perspective that in the process of interaction between systems both are subject to influence and change. While it has been suggested that systems thinking enjoys popularity in the social sciences and the professions because of its emphasis on order and predictability (Hoff, 1989), systems also allow for the disharmony and contradiction that Riegel (1975) asserts are more characteristic of the human experience. Conflict and contradiction between the system and its external environment often promote growth, since the disharmony necessitates resolution of the conflict. For example, early women's rights advocates committed to social justice joined together to gain the right to vote (they became a change-oriented small-group type of system). This led to profound changes in society's thinking regarding women and consequent social-structural and cultural adaptations (that is, changes in the political, legal, and economic systems of society). Sexism remains, however, a significant and destructive attribute of our culture.

Viewing behavioral components in interaction is a difficult task. Our tendency is to see the world in linear and static terms, a view that alternates between focusing on either one or another system (the family or the workplace) rather than looking at the interaction between the two. Linear thinking assumes direct cause-and-effect relationships. Statements such as "people abuse their children because they were abused" are simplistic and can misdirect intervention. Child abuse has no single causative factor. Rather, it involves psychological, cultural, biological, and social-structural dynamics that occur in multiple systems. Linear thinking tends to oversimplify complex issues and thus intervention plans are based on an oversimplified interpretation of the issues. Systems thinking, focusing on the interaction between many forces at multiple levels, helps the professional abandon these linear approaches because it presents the same phenomena in terms of the dynamic relationships between the components in interaction. This is extremely important to the social work profession. Some concrete examples will now be presented to help you understand the systems perspective more clearly, after which we will analyze the components of systems in more detail.

The Human Body as a System

The body is a biological system composed of highly complex and sophisticated parts that interact to create the biological processes that make human life possible. The body itself is composed of systems that work together to sustain life: the circulatory, respiratory, skeletal-muscular, immune, nervous, endocrine, and reproductive systems work together in highly complex ways. All of these systems can affect the functions of the others. Emphysema, a disease that decreases the efficiency of the lungs to exchange gases, will also affect the circulatory system by increasing stress on the heart. In addition, toxins left in the body because of poor exchange of gases can affect all other bodily systems.

The body itself, considered as a system is sustained by substances outside itself—air, food, and water. The quality and availability of these resources affects the functioning of the body and its internal systems. The ingestion, inhalation, or absorption of toxic substances from the environment can have a deleterious effect on the body as well. A mother who drinks alcohol during pregnancy suffers the risk of having a child born with fetal alcohol syndrome. Vietnam veterans exposed to Agent Orange have suffered from neurological disorders and cancer. The care and nurturance of the human body is vital to growth and development. From a systems perspective, then, the human body can be described in terms of its internal components and its relationships with other external systems (the physical world, nonhuman animal life, plant life, and other humans). Life itself is dependent upon the quality of the interaction between the physical and external environmental forces.

The Family as a System

The family is a social system composed of people who interact with each other in patterned ways. A systems perspective views the members of a family not as isolated units but as interacting members. The ways in which they interact are determined by cultural expectations (such as questions about who should raise the children, or who should be the wage earner), socially-structured situations (like social class and minority-majority group membership), and the biological characteristics of the family members themselves (such as physical capabilities).

Other theorists also using a systems perspective look at families from the view of roles of their members. If roles are unclear or are disrupted, family functioning breaks down. A parent, for example, who abdicates the caretaker role to the oldest child causes that child to disrupt her or his normal role as child by placing too much responsibility on its shoulders before it is prepared to assume this burden. The child may exhibit symptoms of stress resulting from this burden. In order to assist the child, a restructuring of the system—helping the adult cope with parental responsibilities more effectively—will have to occur. Here we can see how the family is in turn affected by other systems. The parent may be unable to be an effective parent because of stress caused by chronic poverty and never having learned effective parenting behaviors in one's own family. Enabling the parent to perform more effectively—and hence help the family as a system to function better—may require the intervention of systems like social welfare income maintenance agencies, participation in parent groups, or counseling in a family service agency.

The family also illustrates another characteristic of systems—changing the relationship between the parts changes the reality of the whole. The family as a whole is qualitatively and quantitatively different from its component parts (individuals or sub-grouping of family members). Rearranging the component parts, as happens in divorce or the removal of a family member for hospitalization, military service, marriage, death, and so on, dramatically affects the whole. It isn't that the family functions as before, with the only change being one less person. Instead, the nature of the interaction between the remaining family members is changed. In divorce, for example, one parent may now perform all the parenting activities. This will require adaptation by all the children and other adults in the family system. These changes are likely to have a significant impact on both the family as a whole and on each of its members.

The Community as a System

The family is located geographically and socially within a neighborhood and community. These entities can also be viewed as systems that interact with the individual and the family system. Herbert Gans (1962) in *The Urban Villagers* describes the complex structures and processes involved in the life of an Italian immigrant community in Boston. Gans's study demonstrated that people's lives and behaviors were heavily influenced by the social structure and values of that community. It also showed how powerfully the nature of community life was affected by changes in other systems, especially the economic system of the larger Boston community.

The structure of many communities has changed during the past few years partly because of changes in the economic and transportation systems. The increased availability of transportation, especially the automobile and airplane, the changing nature of the economy away from farming and heavy industry, and the relocation of work and residential settings to suburban areas have all converged to change the nature of employment and interaction patterns in many communities. The effects of these changes are dramatically illustrated by Camden, New Jersey. Previously a thriving industrial community with a mix of ethnic residents, it has been largely abandoned to poor families who have nowhere else to live but among the crumbling remnants of what was previously middle-class housing (Kerr, 1989). When communities deteriorate to the degree that Camden has, the correlates of poverty and geographic isolation include broken families, illness, crime, and drug abuse. The situation in Camden provides a clear example of how the internal dynamics of a community system are powerfully affected by external systems.

The Social Welfare System

The profession of social work is located within the larger social welfare system. It interacts with multiple systems to affect the social functioning of individuals, families, groups, communities, and the society as a whole. Mental health, health care, and economic supports are all systems within the larger social welfare system that interact to provide services to people. Social workers function in all of these subsystems as part of their effort to help people to function more effectively.

As a system, social welfare is a highly organized structure that delivers help in patterned ways. The effectiveness of the help provided depends on internal and external forces. The health care system, for example, has internal structures that are intended to serve specific populations. Clinics administering to low-income people often have a first-come, first-served scheduling plan. As a result, patients often have to wait hours before being seen. Such internal system dynamics strongly affect the quality of care provided and the likelihood that people will utilize the system.

On the other hand, the external systems that fund medical care, such as governmental and private insurance plans, strongly influence the way in which the medical care system functions. This relationship between the external systems that affect social welfare as a total system and the ways in which specific social welfare systems operate exists for all the component parts of social welfare. Here we can see illustrated smaller systems within larger systems (health care within social welfare, social welfare within the government), and how any system (such as health care) has both internal dynamics and relationships with external systems.

The internal structure and processes of systems, as well as the links between systems, help us to describe reality. These dimensions of systems allow us to explain phenomena as complex as human behavior, as we have tried to do in the above examples of different types of systems. Because systems are so important in our effort to understand human behavior, let us now examine the nature of systems in more detail, focusing on boundaries, exchanges, networks, and purpose as important parts of system functioning.

CHARACTERISTICS OF SYSTEMS

Boundaries

A system is an organized collection of activities and resources that exist within definable social and physical **boundaries** (Federico, 1984). The human person, for example, exists within the physically defined body, while the community has both physical (geographical) and social (who interacts with whom) boundaries.

Boundaries regulate the amount of energy (information, resources, people) exchanged between a system and its environment. An *open system* allows a constant interchange in which energy, information, and resources flow freely between the system and its environment. *Closed systems* do not allow the easy exchange of energy, information, and resources across its boundaries. Optimal functioning of systems requires that their boundaries remain fluid and flexible.

The boundaries of a given system need to be open enough to respond to changing environmental conditions so that new energy and information can be incorporated, yet be firm enough to maintain the internal integrity of the system.

Meeting the mental health needs of a community provides an example. The mental health planner must consider the internal and external pressures, such as economic constraints and political reactions, that could make community boundaries more rigid depending on how they are handled. To illustrate, proposed group homes for mentally retarded adults often draw criticism from surrounding residents. In some cases, the community is closed to new information regarding mental retardation, and responses by community residents are often grounded in fear and prejudice. Other communities are able to accept new information and resources so that they can integrate new residents who are mentally retarded into the fabric of community life.

Working with troubled families also may involve attending to family boundaries. Practice experience tells us, for example, that men who abuse their spouses tend to minimize the family's contact with outside systems. In this way they are able to maintain excessive and destructive control over their spouse and children. Parents with teens may face a very different problem—that of maintaining family boundaries. As teens begin the natural process of increasing their independence and distance from the family, they may reject family boundaries completely. Helping teens to learn how to move toward independence while still respecting necessary family boundaries is a parenting task that requires considerable sensitivity.

Seen from a social work practice perspective, the system seeking help is viewed within its environment. Differentiating a system from its environment is an important part of the assessment phase of the helping process, and the concept of boundaries helps in accomplishing this task. In addition to identifying the boundaries of the system itself, any system can also be analyzed in terms of its **subsystems**, smaller systems that exist within larger systems. A hospital's social service unit, for instance, may be analyzed as its own system made up of its own personnel, services, and clients. However, the entire social service unit may itself be part of the larger hospital system that includes many other units—admitting, maintenance, outpatient services, the laboratory, and so on. Even the hospital is a smaller part of a larger system—the community's health care system that would include other hospitals, physicians, home health services, etc. Here we see clearly illustrated the concept of systems within systems. When we analyze systems, the larger system is called the **suprasystem**, while the smaller systems within a larger system are called *subsystems*. Thus, in the example above the social service department is a subsystem of the hospital suprasystem, while the hospital is a subsystem of the health care suprasystem.

The language of systems helps clarify the relationships between the boundaries of a system and its component parts and the relationship between the parts themselves. In the case of the hospital social service unit, one might find that tension and stress between the supervisory staff and the direct service workers—that is, between subsystems (parts of the system)—negatively affect the functioning of the social service department. This has an effect on other systems in the environment of the social service department, such as the nursing department and the quality of service received by individual clients. In this way we can also see how the subsystem (the social service department—has an impact on the suprasystem (the hospital, which may develop a bad reputation in the community).

The concept of boundaries can be readily applied to biological, psychological, and social-structural systems. The biological structures of cells, organs, and the entire human organism, while interdependent, can be isolated as separate subsystems for independent analysis and treatment by demarcating their boundaries such as skin, tissue, and membrane. In the psychological realm, we can draw boundaries to identify discrete personality traits or the total personality system. Social-structural boundaries can be used to delimit family, political, and economic structures as well as to identify group, organization, and community variables. In a similar way, religious, ideational, and value factors serve to create cultural boundaries.

Purpose

In addition to identifying system boundaries, we are also concerned with system **purposes**, survival usually being one of the most important. In order for a system to achieve its goals, balance must be maintained among the components of the system and with the environmental forces interacting with it. The concept of *homeostasis* refers to the regulatory processes through which the system achieves a state of internal and external balance, or equilibrium. Systems always experience a tension between the need for stability and the desirability of change. For example, the perpetuation of welfare policies that do not adequately meet people's needs assures the continuation of the welfare bureaucracy but demonstrates little concern for the well-being of those receiving welfare benefits.

Maintaining the integrity of a system is, in and of itself, not enough. Growth and evolution of new and emerging forms are also characteristics of life. A view of purpose that directs systems to seek change and new experience as well as stability is compatible with social work practice as presented in this text. It is also consistent with the concept of an open system with flexible boundaries. This type of perspective is dramatically illustrated at the biological level by the infinite adaptive arrangements through which the continuation of the species is promoted. Since systems are interrelated (remember our discussion above about subsystems and suprasystems), it is to be expected that they need to respond to changes in their environment if they are to continue to interact successfully.

Attitudes, ideas, and values related to such fundamental human concerns as family life, sex-role identification, the meaning of work, and the existence (or nonexistence) of a deity form the nucleus around which social and cultural purposes are organized. The excerpt from Susan Zuboff's *In the Age of the Smart Machine* (1988) at the end of this chapter demonstrates how human behavior is affected adversely when such a fundamental value as the meaning of work is not fully considered. She shows how efforts by management to rectify hazardous situations at a paper mill led to a decline in worker efficiency and satisfaction. When interviewed, employees expressed a feeling of detachment from their work in that they no longer were physically involved and therefore felt less pride in their workmanship. We can see, then, how a sense of purpose is fundamental to human endeavors, and that purpose goes well beyond mere homeostasis to include changes in response to changing environments.

Exchange

A third characteristic of systems is **exchange**, the process of interaction between the systems through which resources and outcomes are shared. Systems require resources in order to function effectively and achieve their purposes. They may be supplied from within the system or from the external environment (other systems). The resources utilized by systems as part of their goal attainment are called **inputs**. Conversely, **outputs** refer to the products created by systems after inputs have been utilized in the system. The biological process of breathing illustrates the relationship between inputs, processing by systems, and outputs. Human beings (biological systems) inhale oxygen (an input) from the atmosphere (an external system). The lungs absorb the oxygen, which is then distributed to the heart and brain through the blood (the oxygen is processed by the human body system). The system output is energy and life—the ability of the human body to continue to function. A vital aspect of the system is its ability to screen and regulate input. If the regulatory processes fail or are overstressed, the system may be jeopardized. For example, when hyperventilation occurs, breathing becomes too rapid for the body to process all of the oxygen that is inhaled and serious complications can result.

Inputs can be real or imagined. If people interpret situations as real (that is, accept them as inputs), there will be real behavioral consequences (output). Cultural values that glamorize youth, physical appearance, and wealth often affect people's behavior even though there are no actual physiological advantages of these characteristics. Unless people can recognize these values (inputs) for their true worth, they can develop negative self-images (outputs) or engage in behavior that is damaging, such as excessive dieting or undergoing dangerous plastic surgery (also outputs). Part of society's failure to meet the needs of those who have physical shortcomings can be viewed both as a collective denial of the body's fragility and as society's tendency to emphasize productivity over personhood.

We can also see how exchanges occur in larger social-structural systems. The nation's economic system receives inputs in the form of labor contributed by family members (the labor is an output by the family system). This labor is processed to produce products (outputs) that generate income for corporations (inputs for the corporation) from which salaries are paid to working family members (inputs for the family).

Examining exchanges between and across boundaries by biological, psychological, social-structural, and cultural systems aids social work professionals in dynamically interpreting events and phenomena. A wide range of interchanges between different types and sizes of systems becomes more understandable. Understanding the impact of a proposed military base on the economic life of the surrounding community can yield multiple levels of analysis. By looking at such factors as the effect of the base on community housing patterns and the job market, we can see how political and economic systems become part of the environment of family systems. Internal family dynamics are likely to be affected by the availability of jobs and the type of housing available. The behavior of family members will, in turn, affect the larger systems—the availability of skilled workers for the base, for example. This type of perspective provides a holistic view in which subsystems and suprasystems are identified. In addition, the exchanges that provide inputs and that lead to outputs can be identified, and they become significant resources that affect goal identification and goal attainment in the interacting systems.

Networks

A **network** is the means by which exchange occurs between systems. It is established when patterned relationships develop between systems that permit the regular exchange of inputs and outputs (Hanchett, 1979). The educational system, for example, is comprised of a network of public, private, and religious educational systems, each further divided into preschool, primary, secondary, undergraduate, graduate, and trade or business schools. The regular exchange of inputs and outputs that is made possible by networks of systems utilizes the concepts of subsystems and suprasystems discussed earlier.

Networks are established because of shared or related purposes among systems, to ensure the availability of needed inputs, and to coordinate the activities of systems so that they can all survive. The drive in the 1960s to emphasize the sciences in the educational system was directly related to concerns in the political system that the Soviets were winning the space race. Now, during a period of *glasnost* and *perestroika*, such competition is of less concern. However, the educational system is currently becoming more involved with the economic system because of shortages of young workers who are literate and skilled enough to perform increasingly complex jobs.

People participate in many systems throughout their lives. The pregnant teenager, the unemployed factory worker, the disabled mother of three children, and the recently retired business executive are all part of systems joined in networks. To understand each is to understand them in this context: Each person is affected by the systems in which he or she functions, and each system is affected by the other systems in its network. We can see, then, how a systems perspective is multifaceted. It helps us to analyze individual systems as well as systems in interaction, and it alerts us to the fact that there are multiple layers of systems ranging from the individual to large and complex organizations, communities, and societies. Having looked at systems in some detail, let us now examine the other parts of our analytical framework.

DIRECTIONALITY AND MOTIVATION

People do not generally act in a random manner. Milton Erickson (see Bandler & Grinder, 1975) discovered that even the seemingly incoherent verbalizations and actions of schizophrenic patients he treated contained elusive but meaningful content. All behavior is directed toward the attainment of some purpose. The goals people seek may be biological, psychological, social, or cultural. People eat to maintain health, a biological goal, yet what they eat may reflect cultural beliefs about what is healthy and what is fashionable. People sob as a means of expressing emotion, a psychological goal, although crying is in part biologically determined and to some degree a reflection of social and cultural dictates about when such emotional display is appropriate. Employment is sought to meet various goals: biological (the body's need to grow through activity), psychological (the quest for a feeling of competence), social (the need for money to purchase the necessities of life), and cultural (expectations that adults will work and be financially independent).

Personal goals and choices are influenced by multiple factors. People do not formulate their goals independently, nor do they seek only to attain their own personal goals. Many of the systems discussed earlier in the chapter serve to bring people together so as to attain the goals of the larger groups to which they belong. Unions became a powerful force during the late nineteenth and early twentieth centuries in this country when workers began to seek improved economic benefits for themselves. When a group of workers today refuses to cross the picket line set up by another group, they are reaffirming the goals of the larger collective of workers rather than their own immediate goals.

White (1963) and Montessori (1963) both concluded after extensive observations of children that humans possess an innate need to interact and master their environment through meaningful interaction. Competence itself provides intrinsic value to the individual. Refer again to Exhibit 1 at the end of this chapter and reflect on the needs expressed by the workers in the paper mill. It is clear that the quality of the work experience is very meaningful to them, a point that we see in accounts of people who leave high-paying and prestigious jobs for less-well-paid jobs that have more meaning and personal rewards.

Although individual people make the decisions that guide their behavior, they are strongly affected by their access to resources and the obstacles they face. Therefore, when trying to understand an individual's actions, social work practitioners must assess the systems involved in their decision making, including the resources and obstacles they offer and the person's perception of them. Cognitive theory, discussed earlier in the text, helps us to understand that people attribute meaning to the information they receive and the events they experience. One person who does not receive a promotion may view it as a disastrous personal setback, whereas to another it is only a disappointment and motivation to work harder.

Goals often provide clear-cut strategies for action. In order to purchase a home, a young couple must save, cut back on nonessentials, establish good credit, and so forth. To compete in sports, athletes must eat properly, rest, and exercise in prescribed ways. In both of these examples, social structures can either support or inhibit people's achievement of their goals. For example, the young couple's parents can offer to babysit to enable them to save the cost of hiring a sitter. On the other hand, sexist policies may deny women the opportunity to compete in certain sports.

Strategies for attaining other types of purposes may be less clear-cut. To receive love and acceptance from another person requires balancing personal needs with the needs of the other. Problems in relationships arise when this balance is not achieved. Issues of personal privacy, intimacy, careers, and children all call for negotiations between the persons involved (Jordan and others, 1989). Negotiating is a sensitive and delicate process that requires much trial and error, quite different from the relatively straightforward tasks of saving money or maintaining a healthy diet. Here, too, social structures and cultural values can be very important. The availability of social welfare agencies to provide counseling is a resource for people attempting to establish or preserve relationships. On the other hand, cultural values that devalue nontraditional relationships, such as among unmarried homosexual or heterosexual couples, are obstacles (Gutis, 1989).

Personal choices can lead to behaviors that appear self-destructive. For example, adolescents may begin to abuse drugs and alcohol in an effort to find acceptance with peers. Negative consequences may result such as school failure, family problems, and risk of serious injury and failing health. This is where the link between purpose and behavior can seem weak. It may seem odd that people are acting purposefully when what they are actually doing is hurting themselves. Yet this can be the case. Trying to attain one goal sometimes leads to behavior that interferes with other goals.

It would be a mistake to assume that people were acting randomly just because what they were doing was, at least in part, self-defeating. A holistic view is important, as you already know. Once we understand all of the goals that are being sought, we can figure out what behaviors are tied to which goal-directed behaviors. It is then easier to help people learn need-meeting strategies that are more likely to enable them to attain all their goals with minimal adverse effects. In the above illustration, for example, drug abuse would be understood as oriented toward peer acceptance rather than personal weakness or an indication of a death wish. However, using drugs will have negative consequences for the attainment of other goals, such as remaining healthy and completing one's education in preparation for future employment. Therefore, practitioners seek to help adolescents recognize the relationships between their drug use and the probability of reaching all of their goals (a holistic view). This then makes it possible to help them explore alternative strategies that would lead to peer acceptance as well as being healthy and succeeding in school.

Because people have **common human needs**, they create or structure environments to help meet those needs. Social decisions about ways to meet common human needs interact with biological and other natural factors. The "spiritual" need referred to in Chapter 1 is met in Western society through organized and hierarchical churches and is grounded in a sense of community. Conversely, Eastern spirituality is rooted more fundamentally in the personal experiences of universal "oneness" and, although still ritualized, is less community based and hierarchical.

The idea of common human needs serves to link knowledge of systems and directionality. Each type of system has its own particular basic needs that must be met if it is to survive. Because some systems are individual and others are composed of many people, some actions will be individual and others collective (subsystems and suprasystems). A holistic approach requires an understanding of the characteristics of the systems surrounding the person but also their individual understanding and interpretations of their experience. The reasons why common human needs are experienced and interpreted differently leads us to the last part of our analytical framework: human diversity.

HUMAN DIVERSITY

When we look at different strategies utilized by different systems to meet their common human needs and the shared purposes resulting from them, we are not evaluating one as better or worse than another. To do so would be to adopt an ethnocentric point of view that does not value the expression of **human diversity**. This refers to the biological, psychological, social-structural, and cultural ways in which people differ. Chapters 1 and 2 discussed reasons why these differences exist. The genetic inheritance of people makes them different in many ways. As they grow (biological) and have life experiences (social and cultural), their psychological characteristics emerge. People become characterized by high or low intelligence, calm or agitated personalities, and cooperative or competitive relationships with others. They bring their biological and psychological characteristics into their social world, making friends easily or with difficulty, working steadily or moving from job to job, getting married or choosing to remain single.

The individual characteristics and life histories that individuals carry with them interact with the needs and characteristics of the systems in which they function. Sometimes this interaction occurs smoothly, but many times it does not. To understand this interaction, a **dual perspective** is helpful. This suggests that all behavior is viewed in two ways. The first is how people see their own behavior, and the second is how outsiders view the same behavior (Norton, 1978:3–12). People with physical limitations often focus on their abilities rather than their limitations, but they are often viewed by others primarily in terms of their disabilities. When seeking employment, these people may focus on the contributions they can make to an organization while employers may instead emphasize the costs that would be incurred in employing them. To appreciate what happens as these two systems interact (the individual worker and the organization), we must be able to see both points of view. The dual perspective is especially helpful when practitioners are called upon to mediate conflicting system viewpoints.

The Experience of Diversity

The dual perspective allows us to see that people are constantly managing two parts of themselves. As people (individual systems), they develop a sense of identity based on their biological characteristics (pretty or unattractive, smart or average, disabled or able-bodied) and their psychological attributes (loving or aloof, passive or aggressive, altruistic or selfish). In addition, people develop social identities based in their ethnic, racial, gender, sexual orientation, and socioeconomic characteristics. Lower-paid workers, for example, soon see that they are viewed differently from the wealthy owners of the company where they work. Even larger systems develop identities, as when a community is proud of its cleanliness and when the United States cherishes being ''the land of the free.''

These identities become important in two ways. They strongly influence the goals that people (and larger systems) consider appropriate and attainable. When self-identity is positive, it tends to encourage people to take command of their own lives. When it is negative, the effect is often to make people doubt their ability to function effectively. Members of minority groups are frequently victimized by negative self-identities. Aaron Fricke's account of growing up as a gay man is a good example (Fricke, 1981). He describes how, after a childhood that included spontaneous and highly enjoyable sexual encounters with other boys, he became labeled as a ''queer'' in adolescence. Although his behavior had not changed at all, other people's responses to it had. As a result, Fricke changed from a happy child to a troubled and very unhappy teenager. It was only when he started to make contact with other homosexual men, who were able to reinforce his sense of himself as a decent person, that he was able to emerge as an adult with a secure sense of self. During the period when his self-identity was being attacked, however, he withdrew from his former activities and became very isolated. This is quite common for people who believe that they are not valued.

The other way in which identity is important is the effect that it has on members of other groups. The dual perspective alerts us to the fact that people are constantly reacting to the behavior of members of groups of which they are not a part. In other words, some portion of their own identity is formed in relation to those other groups. For instance, some men who believe that women are too "emotional" reinforce their own sense of identity as "strong" by acting unemotionally, or by showing only angry, hostile, or tightly controlled emotions. In this way masculine behavior becomes defined as actions that favor control over negotiation, and dominance over sharing. In the case of relationships between men and women, the actions and attitudes adopted by men to separate themselves from stereotypes of the "feminine" role also lead to oppression of women by men. This process of stereotyping and emphasizing differences is not an uncommon way for groups to establish their own identities, and it often leads to oppression of some groups by others. Identity, then, develops in each system in part through its interaction with other systems.

Once formed, identity influences people's behaviors. Those who are defined as different or inferior because of their racial, ethnic, gender, sexual preference, age, socioeconomic, or physical and mental characteristics are often discriminated against. In turn, members of these groups often come to accept the definitions of others that they are inferior. This affects their sense of well-being and their life goals and behaviors. For example, adults who live in poverty may discourage their children from aspiring to well-paying and secure jobs that require a college education, considering higher education unrealistic. As a result, poverty becomes a **self-fulfilling prophesy** for the children who gradually come to accept it as inevitable. To counteract this tendency of members of oppressed groups to accept their oppression and a self-identity based on assertions of their inadequacy, advocacy groups have formed to enhance the self-respect and social acceptance of these people. The civil rights, Gray Panthers (for the elderly), women's and gay and lesbian pride movements of the last three decades have stimulated a sense of pride and well-being that has led to social change.

Consequences of Human Diversity

The fact that people meet their common needs in different ways—the phenomenon of human diversity—makes existence a somewhat different experience for members of different groups. This happens in two ways. People's **life styles** are affected, the choices they make about how to carry out life tasks. In addition, they experience different **life chances**, their access to basic life-sustaining and life-enriching resources. Life styles are the most visible means of distinguishing between different systems. These include such factors as styles of clothing, family role patterns, entertainment preferences, styles of interaction and task organization, and community architecture. Life styles reflect people's identity and are often a blend of those things a group defines as important along with some of the views of outsiders. Rastafarian males, for example, can be distinguished by long braided hair (dreadlocks). They also follow strict dietary habits in accordance with their religious beliefs. However, their use of marijuana as part of their religious rituals would have to be modified in the United States.

In general, the study and appreciation of life styles is important to the helping professional in at least two ways. The more common is that life styles must be understood if the helper is going to be able to interact effectively with members of diverse groups. Knowing, for example, the importance of the "faith healer" in the Mexican culture can assist a health care professional in working with migrant laborers by helping them strike a balance between their traditional health/faith practices and the medical treatments utilized in the United States.

But life style is also of concern because of its visibility to society at large. The image that people have of groups is heavily influenced by what they see and experience. Corporations, for instance, attempt to create images of themselves through the media. Consider the images presented in the commercials of a large brokerage firm. The stately, conservatively dressed older gentleman quietly but firmly announces, "We make money the old-fashioned way. *We earn it!*" This image of a solid, no-nonsense, hard-working firm is established in the viewer's mind. The importance of group image is seen in the frequent debates over how various groups are presented on television. Are black people portrayed as poor or criminals? Are women always shown as secretaries or housewives? Are the physically disabled presented as pitiable, helpless people? These images do affect how people perceive members of diverse groups and are of concern. Even nations attempt to provide images of themselves as evidenced by President George Bush's call for a "kinder and gentler nation."

When life styles, or images and stereotypes of life styles, are used to characterize members of diverse groups, they can become the basis for restricting life chances through oppression. If you think for a moment about the biological, psychological, social-structural, and cultural sources of diversity, you will realize that any group is characterized by both similarities and differences. Members of a group share the characteristics that define membership in that group. Women share a gender, Puerto Ricans an ethnicity, the elderly a chronological age range, and those with physical limitations barriers to their full physical freedom. However, within each group there is also considerable diversity. Women vary in terms of their race, ethnicity, and age. Puerto Ricans may be of any age and race, the elderly of any socioeconomic and educational level, and those with physical limitations of any gender and ethnicity. Therefore, whatever stereotypes are developed about a group will inevitably be inaccurate because of the variations within the group. As a result, people who are treated according to stereotypes will endure treatment that is often inappropriate.

Any system that stereotypes people or groups, especially for the purpose of disadvantaging them, treats people as categories rather than as individuals. Seen in sociological terms, people occupy many positions simultaneously—mother, wife, Cuban-American, physician, middle-aged adult, and so on. This richness of human biological, psychological, social, and cultural wholeness is violated when people are viewed according to only one of the dimensions. Why, then, do stereotypes develop? They serve the function of distancing people from each other. This sense of distance is often captured by labels that are negative and dehumanizing. Terms like "queer," "nigger," "wop," and "bitch" are all used to devalue people in a very impersonal, dehumanizing way. They are no longer individual people with hopes, needs, abilities, and self-worth. Therefore, it no longer matters how they are treated because they have been defined as unimportant and faceless. They are seen as different and inferior.

The result of stereotyping and labeling is termed **oppression**, the systematic restriction of people's life chances based on institutionalized prejudice and discrimination. In terms of access to all the major categories of life-sustaining and life-enriching resources, members of oppressed groups are disadvantaged. Not only is poverty growing in the United States, but it is also very unequally distributed, with families headed by single women, blacks, and Hispanics more at risk (Day, 1989; *American Family*, 1989a). A recent study of the homeless in Ohio showed that members of minority groups, the severely mentally limited, chronic substance abusers, and those with physical limitations are most affected by poverty (Roth and others, 1988). Blacks of both sexes and women are paid less than white men, a fact that is correlated to the incidence of poverty noted above (*American Family*, 1989b). Low income also correlates with high rates of premature births, low birth weights, conditions of health, and infant mortality rates (Children's Defense Fund, 1989). The reality of these data can be seen daily in slums populated by members of minority groups who are forced to live in substandard housing, go to inadequate schools, endure crime as a part of daily life, are excluded from stable and adequately paying employment, and are tempted to escape these realities through alcohol and drugs.

Stereotyping based on human diversity characteristics becomes even more insidious when it becomes a tool for maintaining existing oppressive social structures. An oft-used tactic of businesses throughout this century was to pit one ethnic group against another in order to stave off unionism. This can be seen in the present-day rhetoric from conservative politicians and business interests who attempt to lay blame for this country's economic woes on the high cost of social programs.

Oppression is not an intellectual concept. It describes day-to-day life that offers illness, danger, discomfort, and hopelessness. It is not something that just happens. It is the result of social-structural arrangements that systematically create an **underclass**, a group of people who are excluded from the mainstream of America's social institutions (Auletta, 1982). And oppression happens because of human diversity in conjunction with ethnocentrism. Even though people share common human needs, the fact that their life styles, the way in which they seek to meet their needs, are different serves to focus on the differences rather than on shared humanity. Rather than viewing these differences as resources rich with opportunities for societal development, they are used to categorize, stereotype, and disadvantage people. Efforts of majority groups to oppress minority groups set the stage for conflict. As noted above, some groups have entered into the struggle to improve their collective position. Many have been successful in terms of a more positive self-identity and greater (but still limited) access to basic resources. For the poor, however, regardless of race or ethnic background, the situation has worsened. Since 1979 the bottom one-fifth of the population of this country has experienced an 18 percent decrease in available income, while the top one-fifth of the population has increased its income by 16 percent (Passell, 1989). As long as oppression continues, conflict will be an ever-present possibility.

When understanding oppression we also should look beyond basic life-sustaining resources. Quality of life is also a dimension of human experience that needs to be addressed. Oppression makes even survival problematic, but the whole idea of human diversity as both natural and a potential resource goes far beyond mere survival. Underlying the idea of cultural pluralism is the belief that different groups have distinctive contributions to make to the whole of society. In other words, they have resources to offer. Oppression blocks these resources, turning them instead into obstacles for members of oppressed groups. Waste is always costly. This is true at the societal level just as much as it is at the personal level. In a world of increasing scarcity, the question must be asked whether our planet can continue to waste the resources that diverse groups offer to the collective human enterprise.

THE COMMITMENT OF PROFESSIONAL HELPERS

To conclude this section on human diversity, a brief look at the impact of the concepts discussed in this chapter on the role of professional helpers is appropriate. In Chapter 1, the purpose of professional social work was defined as helping people to function more effectively by facilitating transactions between them and their environments. Maluccio (1981) suggests that insights from systems theory, the ecological perspective, and competency-based practice provides themes for practice. These include:

1. The view of human organisms as engaged in ongoing, dynamic transactions with their environment, and in a continuous process of growth and adaptation;

2. the conception of people as "open systems" that are spontaneously active and essentially motivated to achieve competence in coping with life demands and environmental challenges;
3. the premise that varied environmental opportunities and social supports are necessary to sustain and promote people's efforts to grow, to achieve self-fulfillment, and to contribute to others;
4. the conviction that appropriate supports should be matched to people's changing qualities and needs so as to maximize the development of individual competence, identity, autonomy, and self-fulfillment.

Social workers need a holistic approach to identify the problematic components of the practice situations with which they work. A holistic assessment that includes biological, psychological, social-structural, and cultural dimensions helps to identify targets of intervention at various system levels. The social work principles of client self-determination and worker competence guide the practitioner in working with and on behalf of client systems.

A holistic view of people in their environment includes the distinctiveness of people as well as the shared tasks faced by all human beings. From biological beginnings that create the limits and potential for individual development, people move into larger systems that increasingly shape their behavior. Unfortunately, this includes various forms of oppression against members of diverse groups that have created millions of troubled individuals. The social and personal problems created by oppression and neglect have become pandemic. Until the environmental systems that deprive people of the life-sustaining and life-enriching resources that they need are changed, individuals will continue to suffer needlessly (Brown, 1984). Social work seeks to eradicate the sources of oppression, to remove obstacles, and to support inherent resources. To do less only perpetuates the problem.

SUMMARY

This chapter has extended the concept of a holistic view of human behavior. We have seen that behavior is organized into systems that exist at many levels, ranging from individual to societal to cultural systems. Each system is concerned with attaining its goals, some of which are shared by similar systems and others that are unique to particular systems. The way purposes and goals are sought reflects the human-diversity characteristics of systems. Interaction between systems sometimes leads to oppression, in which the life chance of members of some systems are methodically restricted by other systems. Oppression is supported by cultural ethnocentric beliefs and social-structural arrangements that result from them, and thus can only be changed by intervention at these levels. However, people's daily lives are affected by oppression, and help is needed at the individual and small-group levels, as well as at the larger systems level.

Focusing on all levels is necessitated by the commitment that social workers share in improving the transactions between people and their environment.

KEY TERMS

Boundary. That which separates a system from its environment. The identifiable limits of a system.

Common human need. A need shared by all human beings and which is basic for survival in a healthy state.

Dual perspective. Understanding the self-view of a population, as well as the view of other groups that evaluate its behavior.

Exchange. The process of interaction between a system and its environment.

Human diversity. Differences between individuals and groups based on biological, cultural, social, and psychological variables.

Input. Internal or external resources of a system.

Life chances. Access to basic life-sustaining and life-enriching resources.

Life style. Choices about how to carry out life tasks.

Model. A way of organizing related concepts and theories.

Network. Aggregations of connecting lines, links, or channels among systems.

Obstacles. Factors that inhibit the definition and the attainment of one's goals.

Oppression. Systematic restriction of people's life chances based on institutional prejudice and discrimination.

Output. Resources that have been processed by a system and transformed into a system product.

Purpose. A goal or desired event.

Resources. Factors that facilitate people's ability to define and achieve life goals.

Self-fulfilling prophesy. Action that assures consequences that will confirm the interpretation of a situation or event by an individual or group.

Subsystem. A component of a larger system.

Suprasystem. A larger system that incorporates smaller systems.

System. A whole that is composed of interrelated and interdependent parts.

Underclass. People who are excluded from the mainstream of the dominant culture's social institutions.

STUDY QUESTIONS

1. Examine the four practice examples that introduce this chapter. How can the integrating framework of systems, human diversity, and directionality help you to understand the common base and the differences among the various examples?
2. Analyze Exhibit 1 at the end of the chapter from a systems perspective. Does such a perspective help or hinder your understanding of the situation and your understanding of human diversity and/or directionality? Explain how it does or does not help.
3. According to the systems approach, change introduced in one part of the system affects changes in other parts of the system and even other systems. What is the implication of this for social work intervention at the individual level? The family level? The community level?
4. Systems perspectives lend themselves easily to graphic representations. Make a diagram in which your class is viewed as a social system. Illustrate its boundaries, and then chart the inputs and outputs exchanged between it and the suprasystems and subsystems that relate to it.
5. Societal resources are allocated through social-structural arrangements encompassing political, economic, and ideational systems. How does the interrelationships between these systems have an impact on the public policy of health care? The role and status of women and minorities?
6. Professionals need to keep in mind that a great deal of diversity exists within any ethnic group. What are some of the variables that account for this fact?
7. People perceive life goals based on the options provided by their culture. What options do contemporary American culture provide women in terms of their career choices? How do these differ from the options provided men? How do they differ from the options provided women twenty-five years ago?

REFERENCES

American Family (1989a). Hispanic Poverty Remains at Near-Recession Levels, and Economic Disparity Gap between Blacks and Whites Widens. Vol. 12, No. 1 (January), pp. 21–22.

American Family (1989b). Equality Between the Sexes: New Studies Create a Stir. Vol. 12, No. 5 (May), pp. 1–3.

Auletta, K. (1982). *The Underclass.* New York: Random House.

Bandler, R. and J. Grinder (1975). *Patterns of the Hypnotic Techniques of Milton H. Erickson, M.D.*, Vol. I. Cupertino, CA: Meta Publications.

Brown, C. (1984). Manchild in Harlem. *New York Times Magazine*, September 16, pp. 36ff.

Carson, R. (1987). *The Silent Spring: 25th Anniversary Edition.* Boston: Houghton Mifflin.

Children's Defense Fund (1989). Latest Child Health Data Spotlight Need for Federal Action. *Children's Defense Fund Reports*, Vol. 10, No. 8 (February/March), p. 3.

Day, P. (1989). The New Poor in America: Isolation in an International Political Economy. *Social Work*, Vol. 34, No. 3, pp. 227–233.

Federico, R. (1984). *The Social Welfare Institution*, 4th ed. Lexington, MA: D. C. Heath.

Fricke, A. (1981). *Reflections on a Rock Lobster*. Boston: Alyson Publishing Co.

Gans, H. (1962). *The Urban Villagers*. New York: Free Press.

Gutis, P. (1989). What Is a Family? Traditional Limits Are Being Redrawn. *New York Times*, August 31, pp. C1ff.

Hanchett, E. (1979). *Community Health Assessment: A Conceptual Tool*. New York: Wiley.

Hoff, L. A. (1989). *People in Crisis: Understanding and Helping*, 3rd ed. Redwood City, CA: Addison-Wesley, p. 13.

Jordan, C., with N. Cobb and R. McCully (1989). Clinical Issues of the Dual-Career Couple. *Social Work*, Vol. 34, No. 1, pp. 29–32.

Kerr, P. (1989). Lingering Death of Camden Imperils Its Healthy Suburbs. *New York Times*, September 7, pp. A1ff.

Maluccio, A. (1981). *Promoting Competence in Clients*. New York: Free Press.

Menninger, K. (1963). *The Vital Balance: The Life Process in Mental Health and Illness*. New York: Viking Press.

Millay, E. St. Vincent (1959). *Collected Sonnets*. New York: Harper & Row.

Montessori, M. (1963). *Education for a New World*. Madras, India: Kalakshetra Publishers.

Norton, D. (1978). *The Dual Perspective*. New York: Council on Social Work Education.

Passell, P. (1989). Forces in Society, and Reaganism, Helped Dig Deeper Hole for Poor. *New York Times*, July 16, pp. 1ff.

Riegel, K. (1975). Toward a Dialectical Theory of Development. *Human Development*, Vol. 18, pp. 50–64.

Roth, D. and others (1988). *Homelessness in Ohio: A Study of People in Need*. Columbus: Ohio Department of Mental Health, Office of Program Evaluation and Research.

Satir, V. (1982). *Conjoint Family Therapy*, 3rd rev. ed. Palo Alto, CA: Science and Behavior Books.

Weick, A. and others (1989). A Strengths Perspective for Social Work Practice. *Social Work*, Vol. 34, No. 4, pp. 350–354.

White, R. (1963). *Ego and Reality in Psychoanalytic Theory*. New York: International Universities Press.

Zuboff, S. (1988). *In the Age of the Smart Machine*. New York: Basic Books.

EXHIBIT 1   THE WORK SYSTEM

The following is taken from In the Age of the Smart Machine: The Future of Work and Power, *by Shoshanna Zuboff. Copyright © 1988 by Basic Books, Inc. Reprinted by permission of Basic Books, Inc., Publishers, New York. It uses the workplace as an example of a system, and provides particular insight into how human values affect the use of technology.*

> We had pleased ourselves with the delectable visions of the spiritualization of labor. . . . Each stroke of the hoe was to uncover some aromatic root of wisdom. . . . But . . . the clods of earth, which we so constantly belabored and turned over and over, were never etherealized into thought. Our thoughts, on the contrary, were fast becoming cloddish. Our labor symbolized nothing and left us mentally sluggish in the dusk of the evening. (Nathaniel Hawthorne, *The Blithedale Romance*)

The Automatic Doors

The bleach plant is one of the most complex and treacherous areas of a pulp mill. In Piney Wood, a large pulp plant built in the mid-1940s, railroad tank cars filled with chemicals used in the bleaching process pull up alongside the four-story structure in which dirty brown digested pulp is turned gleaming white. Each minute, 4,000 gallons of this brown mash flow through a labyrinth of pipes into a series of cylindrical vats, where they are washed, treated with chlorine-related chemicals, and bleached white. No natural light finds its way into this part of the mill. The fluorescent tubes overhead cast a greenish-yellow pall, and the air is laced with enough chemical flavor that as you breathe it, some involuntary wisdom built deep into the human body registers an assault. The floors are generally wet, particularly in the areas right around the base of one of the large vats that loom like raised craters on a moonscape. Sometimes a washer runs over, spilling soggy cellulose knee-deep across the floor. When this happens, the men put on their high rubber boots and shovel up the mess.

The five stages of the bleaching process include hundreds of operating variables. The bleach operator must monitor and control the flow of stock, chemicals, and water, judge color and viscosity, attend to time, temperature, tank levels, and surge rates—the list goes on. Before computer monitoring and control, an operator in this part of the mill would make continual rounds, checking dials and graph charts located on the equipment, opening and shutting valves, keeping an eye on vat levels, snatching a bit of pulp from a vat to check its color, sniff it, or squeeze it between his fingers ("Is it slick? Is it sticky?") to determine its density or to judge the chemical mix.

In 1981 a central control room was constructed in the bleach plant. A science fiction writer's fantasy, it is a gleaming glass bubble that seems to have erupted like a mushroom in the dark, moist, toxic atmosphere of the plant. The control room reflects a new technological era for continuous-process production, one in which microprocessor-based sensors linked to computers allow remote monitoring and control of the key process variables. In fact, the entire pulp mill was involved in this conversion from the pneumatic control technology of the 1940s to the microprocessor-based information and control technology of the 1980s.

Inside the control room, the air is filtered and hums with the sound of the air-conditioning unit built into the wall between the control room and a small snack area. Workers sit on orthopedically designed swivel chairs covered with a royal blue fabric, facing video display terminals. The terminals, which display process information for the purposes of monitoring and control, are built into polished oak cabinets. Their screens glow with numbers, letters, and graphics in vivid red, green, and blue. The floor here is covered with slate-gray carpeting; the angled countertops on which the terminals sit are rust brown and edged in black. The walls are covered with a wheat-colored fabric and the molding repeats the polished oak of the cabinetry. The dropped ceiling is of a bronzed metal, and from it is suspended a three-dimensional structure into which lights have been recessed and angled to provide the right amount of illumination without creating glare on the screens. The color scheme is repeated on the ceiling—soft tones of beige, rust, brown, and gray in a geometric design.

The terminals each face toward the front of the room—a windowed wall that opens onto the bleach plant. The steel beams, metal tanks, and maze of thick pipes visible through those windows appear to be a world away in a perpetual twilight of steam and fumes, like a city street on a misty night, silent and dimly lit. What is most striking about the juxtaposition of these two worlds, is how a man (and there were only men working in this part of the mill) traverses the boundary between them.

The control room is entered through an automatic sliding-glass door. At the push of a button, the two panels of the door part, and when you step forward, they quickly close behind you. You then find yourself facing two more automatic doors at right angles to one another. The door on the right leads to a narrow snack area with booths, cabinets, a coffee machine, and a refrigerator. The door to the left leads into the control room. It will not open until the first door has shut. This ensures that the filtered air within the control room is protected from the fumes and heat of the bleach plant. The same routine holds in reverse. When a man leaves the control room, he presses a button next to the frame on the inner door, which opens electronically. He then steps through it into the tiny chamber where he must wait for the door to seal behind him so that he can push a second button on the outer door and finally exit into the plant.

This is not what most men do when they move from the control room out into the bleach plant. They step through the inner door, but they do not wait for that door to seal behind them before opening the second door. Instead, they force their fingertips through the rubber seal down the middle of the outer door and, with a mighty heft of their shoulders, pry open the seam and wrench the door apart. Hour after hour, shift after shift, week after week, too many men pit the strength in their arms and shoulders against the electronic mechanism that controls the door. Three years after the construction of the sleek, glittering glass bubble, the outer door no longer closes tightly. A gap of several inches, running down the center between the two panels of glass, looks like a battle wound. The door is crippled.

"The door is broke now because the men pushed it too hard comin' in and out," says one operator. In talking to the men about this occurrence, so mundane as almost to defy reflection, I hear not only a simple impatience and frustration but also something deeper: a forward momentum of their bodies, whose physical power seems trivialized by the new circumstances of their work; a boyish energy that wants to break free; a subtle rebellion against the preprogrammed design that orders their environment and always knows best. Yet these are the men who also complained, ''The fumes in the bleach plant will kill you. You can't take that chlorine no matter how big and bad you are. It will bleach your brains and no one (in management) gives a damn.''

Technology represents intelligence systematically applied to the problem of the body. It functions to amplify and surpass the organic limits of the body; it compensates for the body's fragility and vulnerability. Industrial technology has substituted for the human body in many of the processes associated with production and so has redefined the limits of production formerly imposed by the body. As a result, society's capacity to produce things has been extended in a way that is unprecedented in human history. This achievement has not been without its costs, however. In diminishing the role of the worker's body in the labor process, industrial technology has also tended to diminish the importance of the worker. In creating jobs that require less human effort, industrial technology has also been used to create jobs that require less human talent. In creating jobs that demand less of the body, industrial production has also tended to create jobs that give less to the body, in terms of opportunities to accrue knowledge in the production process. These two-sided consequences have been fundamental for the growth and development of the industrial bureaucracy, which has depended upon the rationalization and centralization of knowledge as the basis of control.

These consequences also help explain the worker's historical ambivalence toward automation. It is an ambivalence that draws upon the loathing as well as the commitment that human beings can experience toward their work. Throughout most of human history, work has inescapably meant the exertion and often the depletion of the worker's body. Yet only in the context of such exertion was it possible to learn a trade and to master skills. Since the industrial revolution, the accelerated progress of automation has generally meant a reduction in the amount of effort required of the human body in the labor process. It has also tended to reduce the quality of skills that a worker must bring to the activity of making something. Industrial technology has been developed in a manner that increases its capacity to spare the human body, while at the same time it has usurped opportunities for the development and performance of skills that only the body can learn and remember. In their treatment of the automatic doors, the bleach plant workers have created a living metaphor that reflects this ambivalence toward automation. They want to be protected from toxic fumes, but they simultaneously feel a stubborn rebellion against a structure that no longer requires either the strength or the know-how lodged in their bodies.

The progress of automation has been associated with both a general decline in the degree of know-how required of the worker and a decline in the degree of physical punishment to which he or she must be subjected. Information technology, however, does have the potential to redirect the historical trajectory of automation. The intrinsic power of its informating capacity can change the basis upon which knowledge is developed and applied in the industrial production process by lifting knowledge entirely out of the body's domain. The new technology signals the transposition of work activities to the abstract domain of information. Toil no longer implies physical depletion. ''Work'' becomes the manipulation of symbols, and when this occurs, the nature of skill is redefined. The application of technology that preserves the body may no longer imply the destruction of knowledge; instead, it may imply the reconstruction of knowledge of a different sort.

The significance of this transposition is impossible to grasp without reference to the grounds of knowledge for workers in the past. In the factory, knowledge was intimately bound up with the efforts of the laboring body. The development of industrial technology can be read as a chronicle of attempts to grapple with the body's role in production as a source of both effort and skill and with the specific responses these attempts have evoked from workers and managers. The centrality of the body's historical meaning for production has informed the self-understanding of managers and workers and the relationship between them. It has also been a salient force guiding the development and application of manufacturing technology. A better understanding of what the body has meant for industrial work and how it has been linked to the logic of automation will sharpen an appreciation of the character of the current transformation and its capacity to provoke comprehensive change in the relationships that structure the workplace. Before deciphering the present or imagining the future, it is first necessary to take ourselves out of the twentieth century and return, if only briefly, to a time when the nature of work was both simpler and more miserable, a time when work was above all the problem of the laboring body.

CHAPTER 4

Human Behavior throughout the Life Course

Life is complex, it changes, and my world was destined to change with it.
Loren Eiseley

CHAPTER OVERVIEW

Each of us comes into the world with a unique genetic makeup. This genetic potential, however, unfolds in a larger social-cultural and historical context. Our individual stories, or autobiographies, as Loren Eiseley suggests, are shaped and formed in interaction with the biographies of others at a given time in history. As you have learned in previous chapters, the study of human behavior does not belong to the exclusive province of any one discipline but involves the interplay of biological, psychological, social-structural, and cultural forces played out in a historical context. Literature and history, especially through the biographical and autobiographical accounts of individuals as they progress through life at any given point, contribute much to our understanding of the richness of human behavior. This interplay of individual biography with social and historical processes is known as the **life course**, defined by Clausen (1986) as "progression through time."

From conception to death, human behavior is shaped by a combination of internal and external factors. Some of these are predictable and are regulated by social norms that give direction and guidance to the individual. In American society, for example, chronological age is often accompanied by changes in status and role transitions reflecting culturally "appropriate" times to begin school, drive a car, start a family, or retire. While there is considerable variability in the timing of these specific life events, individuals internalize "social clocks" and often gauge their progression through the life course accordingly. Parents express concern, for instance, if their 2-year-old hasn't started to talk or if their 23-year-old shows no signs of occupational direction. Questions related to one's "on-timeness" thereby become charged with emotional intensity.

As Rindfuss, Swicegood, and Rosenfeld (1987) point out, however, life events are not always so predictably sequenced. Disruptions and disorders are common occurrences throughout the life course. An unplanned and unwanted pregnancy, the sudden onset of a disease, the loss of a job, a natural catastrophe such as a hurricane or flood all create disorder and disruption in the timing of life events. They require coping strategies that differ from those needed to meet the demands of predictable and anticipated transitions throughout the life course.

This chapter will focus on human behavior throughout the life course. It begins by looking at the concept of the life course, followed by an analysis of the interaction of social and historical forces on life-course dynamics. It also discusses the variables influencing life events. From conception to death, behavior is shaped by societal expectations, subcultural values, historical events, and one's individual goals and aspirations. Each factor that shapes behavior does so by means of the resource systems discussed in the previous chapter. The result is a progression through life according to a type of life course "master plan" that is partly biological, partly psychological, partly social-structural, and partly cultural.

This master plan is frequently disrupted by unanticipated events and occurrences that necessitate a reordering and restructuring of one's life goals. Understanding this master plan, its variations, and its interruptions enables helping professionals to see how the timing, sequencing, and predictability or nonpredictability of life events affect intervention efforts. This view also ties life events to the resources available to address them. This chapter further emphasizes the impact of human-diversity variables during the life course. It will examine how ethnicity, gender, sexual orientation, and physical ability influence behavior throughout the life course. Exhibits at the end of the chapter demonstrate the special concerns of women at midlife who are charged with caring for elderly parents (a need brought about by demographic shifts) and teenagers coming to terms with their sexuality during the age of AIDS. A third Exhibit examines the world of adolescent girls and explores the impact of gender on their development.

DEFINING THE LIFE COURSE

The terms *life cycle* and *life course* are often used interchangeably. Hagestad and Neugarten (1985:35) state that a life-course perspective shifts one's attention from the biological unfolding of one's potential to a concentration on "age related transitions that are socially created, socially recognized, and shared.'' Hareven (1982) views the life course as ''concerned with the timing of life events in relation to the social structures and historical changes effecting them'' (p. xiv).

The concept of the life course is an easy one to understand. It refers to the period from conception through death, encompassing the totality of the physical, psychological, social-structural, and cultural experiences of life at a given time in history. Seen as a whole, the life course represents the aspirations people have about the potential of human life. Parents dream that their children will be happy and successful (however that is defined in a particular culture). In the United States, children often dream that they will be rich and famous. Even cultures and societies nurture collective dreams about what each generation can accomplish to improve the quality of life on this planet. These dreams serve to motivate people, both individually and collectively, in their efforts to move through the life course. Naturally, dreams do not always come true, but dreams die hard and they provide powerful incentives for human behavior.

Age-Graded, History-Graded, and Non-normative Influences on the Life Course

Before examining the life course in detail, let us consider some additional influences on human behavior that help explain the complexity of person-environment transactions. Figure 6 represents the influence of age-graded,

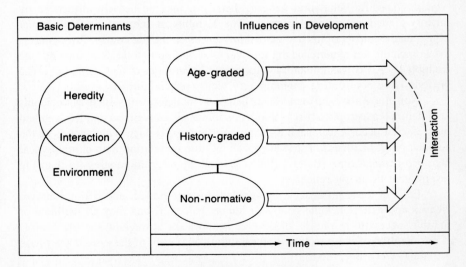

Figure 6. Influences on the Life Course

history-graded, and non-normative events throughout the life course (Baltes, 1987).

Included in **age-graded influences** are those aspects of development related to chronological age (i.e., birth, puberty) as well as age-specific societal expectations (i.e., schooling, retirement). The development theories of Freud, Erikson, and Piaget, presented earlier in this text, illustrate perspectives on human behavior rooted in age-graded changes throughout the life course. These events are usually anticipated and, although, as we will point out later in the chapter, they show some variation, there is enough uniformity throughout a specific culture to allow some agreement within that culture as to the developmental tasks expected at a given point in the life course. Because of the normative and predictable nature of many of these events, advance preparation through anticipatory socialization is often possible (Hagestad and Neugarten, 1985). Anticipatory socialization refers to the ways in which people are prepared for roles that the culture assumes they will perform. For example, girls are encouraged to play with dolls in preparation for their expected adult role of mother. Brim and Rytt (1980) point out that peers provide each other with social support that lessens the potential stress of predictable age-graded life course transitions.

History-graded influences involve societal changes brought about by historical events such as demographic shifts, technological changes, and employment rates. People who are born at about the same time and share similar historical experiences are called **cohorts**. The concept of cohort is useful in explaining history-graded influences at various points in the life course. The men and women who served in the military during the Vietnam War, for instance, probably experience the role of veteran differently from veterans of previous wars. A specific behavioral pattern, therefore, may be heavily influenced by history-graded or cohort variables. The Exhibits at the end of this chapter illustrate the impact of history-graded influences on the life course. Prior cohorts of women did not experience the same tasks at midlife as today's women do (see Exhibit 1). AIDS was not an issue for earlier generations of teenagers, but it is a serious issue confronting contemporary teens (see Exhibit 2).

Non-normative influences on behavior include events such as accidents and natural catastrophes (fires, floods, earthquakes) as well as unanticipated and unpredicted occurrences such as winning a lottery, sudden widowhood, or the sudden onset of illness. These events show little correlation with chronological age or historical time (Baltes, 1987:175) and are often more stressful than life events that occur on schedule.

Each of these influences, age-graded, history-graded, and non-normative, shapes and determines the course of human behavior, and they all facilitate or inhibit successful resolution of developmental tasks throughout the life course. Consideration of these factors is an essential component of the assessment phase of social work intervention.

Life Events and the Life Course

Danish, Smyer, and Nowak (1980) have identified a number of events that occur throughout the course of human life that help us understand human behavior and plan appropriate intervention strategies. Life events are occasions in a person's existence that signal significant milestones or transition points. Marriage and retirement are two such examples. Both are age-related transitions that are accompanied by new role expectations. Life events are not, however, isolated phenomena. They occur in a larger context and are influenced by other events in the individual's life and in the systems in which people live. An approach to the life course that focuses on **critical life events** is consistent with the health model of social work intervention presented in this text. Such a perspective emphasizes continuous growth and change throughout life. It is also consistent with a systems perspective. Critical life events are not viewed as pathological, but rather as occasions that invite growth.

Danish and others (1980) delineate the following properties common to all life events: event-timing, duration, sequencing, cohort specificity, contextual purity, and probability of occurrence. Let us take a brief look at each of these characteristics and examine how they might influence behavior at various points throughout the life course.

Event Timing. The timing of an event may be more significant than the event itself. Did the event occur at a time consistent with social expectations? Marriage at 25 and retirement at 65 are congruent with societal expectations. First marriages at 50 and retirement at 40 are culturally "off time." As pointed out earlier, events that are on time are more likely to gain cultural approval and support than events occurring "off time." Clearly the timing of events is a culturally dependent variable. As culture changes, so too do the ideas regarding societal expectations related to "age-appropriate" behaviors. Today, for example, more people are choosing to delay marriage until they are firmly rooted in their occupational sphere. Others choose not to marry at all, and in selecting either option they are less likely to incite negative sanctions than might have been expected by previous age cohorts.

Duration. This refers to the length of time an event is experienced. Danish and others (1980) suggest it may be helpful to view some events as *processes*, rather than as single occurrences. The duration of the event then includes anticipation of the event, the event itself, and post-event occurrences. The birth of a baby, for instance, involves not only the birth but also the entire course of pregnancy and experiences of early infancy. A career change may involve months of agonizing decision making and often includes consultation with a host of professionals for exploration of career options. In such a scenario the impact of a job change is qualitatively different from the sudden and unplanned loss of employment.

Event Sequencing. Have the events occurred in the socially expected and sanctioned order? Having a child before marriage is not consistent with the culturally prescribed courtship, marriage, and family pattern of family development held by the traditional normative system. Individuals often form their own expectations regarding their personal and/or career paths. A call to military service, for example, may disrupt the personal goals the individual has established for himself. The successful completion of life tasks is usually facilitated if the tasks are supported by cultural expectations and if people have planned for them. As with event timing, the past two decades have witnessed considerable changes in event sequencing.

Cohort Specificity. Events have different meaning for different age cohorts. Living together before marriage today does not usually bring the same negative social sanction that it would have to young couples in the 1950s.

A phenomenon referred to as the **boomerang generation** has gained popular attention recently. This refers to young adults choosing to return to their parental home after living independently for some time. This move is often the result of economic necessity, but as it becomes common in the population (i.e., cohort specific) it is viewed by the larger culture more as an adaptive behavior than as a personal failure.

Contextual Purity. **Contextual purity** refers to the degree that one event interferes with other events occurring at the same time. When an event happens at an otherwise uneventful time in one's life, it is considered contextually pure. Events also influence, as pointed out above, the lives of others. For the purpose of intervention it is essential to consider how a specific event enhances or inhibits successful resolution of other developmental tasks in one's life or in the life of others.

Human beings do not live their lives in isolation. Their lives are entwined with those of their family, their friends, and the larger community. Any setting in which we find ourselves is populated by participants at different developmental stages. Families, for example, are composed of individuals at different developmental stages. Think of Exhibit 1 at the end of the chapter regarding women at midlife (and increasingly in later life) providing the care-giving function for their aging parents. If the caregiver's life is relatively stable and otherwise uneventful, caring for aging parents could be considered contextually pure. In such a scenario, that added task may not be as stressful as it would be were the caregiver confronted with conflicting developmental issues. This is often the case if women work to help support the family, of if they are still caring for young children. It should be pointed out that men also assume caretaking responsibilities for aging parents, as the Exhibit makes clear. The concept of contextual purity is also useful for understanding their behavior.

Probability of Occurrence. This relates to the likelihood that a specific event will be experienced by a large proportion of the population. Age-graded normative influences discussed in the previous section have a high probability of occurrence. These are often referred to as *normative life crises* (Ginsberg, 1975). The non-normative influences on development discussed in a preceding section have a low probability of occurrence. To the extent that events have a high probability of occurrence, it is possible to prepare in advance for them. Community support systems and educational programs (preretirement seminars, for example) can be designed to ease the impact of the event itself or the after-effect of the event.

Events with low probability of occurrence (discussed earlier in the chapter as non-normative influences) are unplanned and unanticipated. Their impact on the individual or the population affected are qualitatively different and require different coping strategies in response. The San Francisco earthquake of 1989, for instance, demonstrated a community well prepared for such a catastrophe. Even so, thousands were left homeless. Such a disaster clearly disrupts the life course of those both directly and indirectly affected.

Understanding the impact of both anticipated and unanticipated life events in terms of their timing, duration, sequencing, cohort specificity, contextual purity, and probability of occurrence helps us view the life course holistically. It is consistent with the person-in-situation perspective and the health model of social work presented throughout this text.

Stages in the Life Course

Dividing the life course into distinct periods, each with its characteristic problems and potentials, has captured the imagination of artists and scientists throughout human history. Shakespeare, in *As You Like It*, presents seven stages of human development that closely parallel Erikson's developmental stages presented in Chapter 2. Others, through the use of metaphor, compare the stages of life with the seasons of the year. Spring is the time of youth and promise; summer the time of adulthood and greatest productivity; autumn the time of harvest and transition to later life; and winter the period of old age and decline (Kimmel, 1980). Covey (1989), through analysis of art and literature, has demonstrated how stages of life were viewed in the Middle Ages. Social scientists have recently, however, begun to question the validity of viewing the life course as unfolding in a one-directional manner in which each successive stage flows from and builds on the previous stage in a neatly packaged sequential order. Periods of growth and decline are closely intertwined. Germain (1987) believes stage theories reflect a too rigid and linear view of the course of human life and are not congruent with the transactional view of behavior that characterizes contemporary scientific thought.

From a purely biological perspective, human development occurs in a carefully sequenced manner—early childhood, for instance, is a period marked by the development of motor coordination skills, adolescence is a time of rapid hormonal change, and later life witnesses decrements in all five of the senses. These changes occur throughout the species with minimal influence of culture. They are universal and show little variation. Biological development, however, as has been emphasized throughout this book, occurs in a psycho-social-cultural-historical context. The developmental stages presented in this chapter are merely ways of conceptualizing these multiple sources and influences on behavior in terms of their interaction. As each stage is presented, specific developmental tasks accompanying the stage will be considered. These tasks are culturally defined and translated through social structures into expected behaviors.

Viewing the life course in terms of stages with stage-specific developmental tasks is simply a tool to help you view human life as a totality of biological, psychological, cultural, and social-structural factors. Any attempt to view these stages and their related tasks as occurring in a non-variant pattern to all members of the population ignores the richness of human diversity. Throughout the discussion that follows we will look at the obstacles and resources related to each stage, comment on possible influences (history-graded, non-normative, and life events) and suggest implications for intervention. Table 5 graphically presents this framework.

The remainder of this chapter will focus on the following stages in the life course: conception and birth, infancy and early childhood (birth to about age 4), middle and late childhood (from about 4 to 12), adolescence (from about 13 to 18), young adulthood (18 to 35), middle adulthood (35 to 55), later adulthood (55 to 75), and old age (75 and older).

Conception and Birth as a Life Stage

Tasks. Conception and birth is a period of expansion for individuals, groups, and society. For the individual (the parent), the self becomes the source of life for others. This generally adds to one's sense of competence, continuity, and importance, although it also increases one's responsibilities. For specific groups

TABLE 5. A FRAMEWORK FOR ANALYZING THE LIFE COURSE

Factors Affecting the Life Course Tasks

Resources and Obstacles	Influences	Variations
Biological	Age-graded	Gender
Psychological	History-graded	Ethnicity
Social-structural	Non-normative	Physical abilities
Cultural	Life events	Sexual orientation

and for society as a whole, conception and birth ensure the survival of the social unit by replacing members and even increasing the size of the unit. The focus during this **life stage** is on decision making and preparation for new life. The decision to have a child is a significant one for the individuals directly involved. It engages a network of interpersonal relationships that will be used to provide emotional and financial support during the pregnancy and after the child is born. Groups impinge on individual decision making through cultural definitions of the desirability of pregnancy and the conditions under which it should occur. Groups also form the support structures that provide the context in which conception and birth occur.

Biological tasks focus on the reproductive act and the physical and emotional conditions needed for a healthy pregnancy and a secure birth. Psychological tasks relate to the readiness of the partners involved to conceive and to carry a child. This includes a sense of well-being about oneself and the baby, knowledge about conception, pregnancy, and birth, and the existence of emotional support systems. Social-structural tasks pertain to creating or finding an environment in which conception can occur by choice and the pregnancy and birth can take place in a safe context. Cultural tasks are those that engage belief and value systems to support the parents and the child. Together, these four task areas attempt to provide for the emotional and physical life-sustaining needs of the child and its parents. This includes the creation of a receptive social context in which the child will be able to grow and develop.

The life stage of conception and birth is unique in that during it, the person being conceived and born is completely dependent on others. Conception itself is the result of decisions and actions by others that precede the person-to-be. Conditions under which the fetus develops are also strongly influenced by others, particularly the biological parents. The task of the fetus itself—to develop physically and to survive—is engaged through its genetically inherited developmental potential. Thus, for the fetus the task is almost exclusively physiological. The developmental tasks of the fetus, therefore, can be considered as age-graded tasks.

The social, psychological, and cultural factors involved relate to the other people involved in the environment of the fetus. The biological mother is, of course, of particular importance. Consider the contextual purity in which the critical life event of having a child occurs. Is it an otherwise uneventful time for the parent/caregiver? Even the birth process is heavily affected by others. The fetus has its own physiological tasks to perform in the birth process, but the environment into which the fetus emerges is determined by others. For example, even if a doctor diagnosed that a cesarean section would be needed for a safe delivery, the parents would have to initiate the decisions and actions to make it possible. Birth complications are examples of non-normative life events.

This life stage is a good example of the fact that the tasks faced by individuals at various life stages affect each other. The task of the fetus is to grow and survive, although the likelihood of this happening is strongly influenced by the life-stage tasks of the biological parents. Are the parents unmarried adolescents or financially secure married adults? In other words, is the timing and sequencing of this life event congruent with the life-course plans of the parents? The readiness of biological parents to see a fetus through pregnancy, birth, and infancy is an important influence on the new person's ability to carry out his or her own life task. The tasks accompanying conception and birth as a life stage are dependent on both age-graded and non-normative influences. The very decision to have or not to have a child is partly determined by history-graded (cohort) influences. Reproductive technology presents different options to today's parents and potential parents than it did to cohorts only a generation ago.

Resources. Biological resources are those that increase the probability that the mother and child will be healthy. These include the mother's age at conception, her previous pregnancy history, her health, and whether she is addicted to any chemical substances. In general, women between the ages of about 16 and 35 run the least risk of complications during pregnancy. Women who are healthy—that is, who are disease-free and receive proper nutrition—who have not had pregnancy difficulties in the past, and who are not dependent on any drugs or chemical substances are not likely to encounter biological difficulties during pregnancy. The age, nutritional level, and health of the father are also relevant to the biological processes of conception and pregnancy. Finally, the genetic composition of both parents is an important determinant of the course of a pregnancy and birth.

Psychological resources are those that help individuals decide whether they wish to have a child and whether they have the emotional and financial means to do so. This includes knowledge about parenthood, conception, pregnancy, and birth—knowledge basic to informed decision making that will ultimately relate to one's sense of readiness for parenthood. Personality variables are also important. A sense of personal well-being and strength and the ability to confront new situations help people adjust to the demands of pregnancy and parenthood. Willingness to share with others and the ability to cope effectively with physical and emotional stress are also beneficial.

Social-structural resources are those factors that provide concrete help for pregnant women and new parents, as well as social-structural conditions that serve to validate one's changed identity as a parent. Tax benefits for children, health insurance to pay for the medical costs of pregnancy and birth, and company policies that allow a woman to take leave during pregnancy are all significant resources. Additional social-structural resources include the quality of medical care available, social rituals such as baby showers that allow family and friends to express their support, availability of information about conception and parenthood, and personal and genetic counseling. A direct relationship exists between minority-group membership and the availability of these socioeconomic resources (Harper, 1990). Social-structural resources are generally less available to the poor and to members of minority groups.

Cultural resources are those that allow for group approval for conception and birth and that provide a knowledge context for these activities. Being the proper age and having appropriate marital status as defined by one's own group places pregnancy in an acceptable value framework that will lead to social praise and support. The culture, in other words, dictates the proper timing and sequencing for the life event of having a child. Using socially acceptable means of prenatal care, following prescribed sex-role behaviors, and utilizing prevailing beliefs and values that support conception, pregnancy, and birth are also important. Of course, each cultural group has its own definitions of whether conception is desirable, and if so, how it should be managed.

Obstacles. Obstacles are those factors that increase the biological and psychological risks of conception and birth and detach people from the usual social-structural and cultural supports at this life stage. Biological obstacles would include a woman being either very young or old at time of conception, or having a history of pregnancy complications. Other biological obstacles might include the presence of venereal disease in either partner, substance abuse or dependency by the mother, or the existence of genetically transmitted conditions in either partner. Psychological obstacles might be having to adjust to an unwanted child or possessing very limited knowledge of conception, pregnancy, and birth. Another psychological obstacle would be feelings of severe inadequacy by either partner in terms of taking on parenting responsibilities.

Examples of social-structural obstacles would be inadequate financial resources to pay for necessary medical treatment or to provide proper nutrition for the mother; or abusive physical conditions that threaten the mother's needs (a factor that is especially important if there is a complication during pregnancy or at birth). Additional social-structural obstacles would include lack of information about conception, pregnancy, and parenthood, and the lack of available counseling to help those who are struggling with factors related to conception. As noted earlier, poverty is directly related to physical well-being. Therefore, biological and social-structural resources/obstacles are closely associated, because poverty results from economic and political variables. Cultural obstacles are those beliefs and values that devalue conception and birth. A pregnancy occurring "off time" or out of the culturally sanctioned sequence creates obstacles to both parents and child.

Implications for Intervention. Conceiving a child is a major life event. For many it involves a decision that requires as much information and emotional support as possible. It is often a decision shared with significant others, such as family and friends, who can be critical elements in the decision. For some, conception is not decided; it simply happens. This often reflects lack of information about basic physiological processes. In other cases, conception is considered a natural part of life and accepted whenever it occurs. And for still others, it is a decision made to achieve other goals such as a sense of intimacy with another, a feeling of personal importance, or a sense of independence. Professionals have to be able to disentangle the many factors that may be involved in conception in order to provide appropriate resources.

Pregnancy is a time of physical and emotional changes and adjustments. The pregnant woman needs as much information as possible about her pregnancy and a great deal of support as she adjusts her activities and emotions to it. Many women also need financial aid, housing, and other supports so that adequate nutrition and physical care are available. Others involved in the pregnancy, especially the father, also need to be supported and informed. When the pregnancy threatens to lead to exclusion from supporting social structures—such as school, family, work, and so on—efforts should be made to strengthen these linkages or find alternatives. The existence of conditions that threaten the physical well-being of the mother or child—such as drug addiction, disease, illness, or genetic factors—demands a thorough analysis of the implications so that appropriate intervention can be taken.

There are a host of concerns that professionals can anticipate at this life stage. As we have seen, the need for information, for physical care and for medical care, for help in decision making, and for solidifying linkages with support systems are especially critical. In addition, basic life-sustaining resources may be needed, such as money, food, and shelter. The fact that this life stage usually leads to alterations in established life patterns often creates the need for counseling in one or more of the multiple systems that may be involved. For many people, creating new life is a happy, exciting adventure. For others it is quite routine. Still others approach it with fear, anxiety, and a sense of desperation. Professionals must be able to anticipate and respond to all these possibilities so that the newly conceived person can have the best possible chance of meeting its basic task at this life stage—physical development and survival.

In summary, if both the timing and the sequencing of conception and birth are culturally sanctioned, and if these events occur at a time that is relatively free from serious problems for both parents and family (i.e., is contextually pure), professional intervention may not be necessary. The mobilization of the supportive community of family and friends may be all that is indicated.

If, however, conception and birth occur off-time or are out of sequence with either the culturally prescribed pattern or the individual's own life-course plan, professional intervention may be required. In this instance, a variety of roles are appropriate for the generalist practictioner. Early identification of at-risk populations requires skills in case finding. After the populations are identified, special referral skills may be needed to get potential users to appropriate resources. Often, however, resources are not available, in which event skills are needed in mobilizing new resources.

Another common problem is that resources may be there but barriers (such as rigid eligibility requirements) may inhibit their use. In this instance professionals need to develop skills in advocacy, both for the benefit of the individual potential user and for the entire population of users. Knowledge about the person-environment transactions at each stage of the life course, therefore, informs not only daily practice interventions but also policy making.

Infancy and Early Childhood as a Life Stage

As defined here, infancy and early childhood make up the period from birth to about 4 years of age. Infancy is a period that involves the infant and those around it, so the tasks at this stage reflect a range of individuals. For purposes of simplicity, however, we will focus only on the child at this point. The birth and parenting of a child by the adult will be discussed later.

The child is born completely dependent upon the adult caregivers for its survival and growth. Adequate food, shelter, and emotional bonding are required if the infant is to mature biologically, mentally, and emotionally. The child gradually matures biologically, gaining increasing mastery over his or her own limbs, bodily functions, perceptual abilities, and communication mechanisms. Provided a secure and loving environment, the child is initially able to develop trusting relationships with caregivers and later extend this trust to larger circles of individuals. Children must begin the long process of moving in the direction of independence and separation from parental figures.

Resources. The biological resources of the infant are its genetic endowments. Reflexes, neurological mechanisms, skeletal structure, and basic health make it possible for the infant gradually to perceive, organize, and master its environment. The degree of development and mastery will, of course, reflect the nature of the child's genetic equipment. An infant's physical attractiveness, as defined culturally, is also an important biological resource.

Psychological resources in the infant are closely tied to biological endowments. Biological needs in interaction with the social environment produce the psychological resources available to the child. An infant whose needs are met consistently, promptly, and with care will usually develop personality resources that increase the probability of continued growth and strength. Scientists have demonstrated through the study of micro-movements of parent and child that many inherited physical and verbal cues are exhibited by both parent and child which stimulate positive feelings resulting in strong emotional ties between them. Social and physical stimulation will enable the infant to develop its perceptual and cognitive capacities, as well as its ability to relate happily to others. Parents' resources include their receptivity and feelings toward the infant.

Also considered valuable resources that enhance the child's development are the parent's knowledge of infant and child development, which allows parents to provide a nurturing and stimulating environment. Mature parents who can respond to the many changes in their lives demanded by the child's varying needs will also be resources for the child. A sense of competence, closely allied with emotional maturity, allow parents the confidence to undertake the difficult and uncertain tasks of childrearing.

Social-structural resources for the infant are those that enhance its survival and growth. The family, however defined, is the emotional cradle of the infant. The family constellation provides the infant's first contact with the social world. Stability of the family is, therefore, of great importance in the child's development. The nature of medical care, availability of safe housing, heathful nutrition, and adequate formal and informal child-care arrangements are examples of sound social-structural resources. These are also of importance to parents because their availability relieves them of stresses that may interfere with the parent-child relationship. These social-structural resources are necessary throughout childhood, although their form may change as the youngster grows older.

Culturally, the infant benefits from beliefs and values that define children as desirable. Whereas large families are seen as desirable and even necessary in agrarian cultures, industrialization has made the smaller family the norm because it is more adaptable to a wage economy and geographic mobility (a history-graded influence). Culture also defines how we view children and consequently how the infant and child should be reared. Present-day definitions of childhood in the United States are quite different from those during the early part of this century. At that time "persons" at the age of 7 were expected to join the labor force to assist in the financial stability of the household. Now, childhood is extended well into the teenage years, and full-time work is not generally expected until the age of 18 or beyond. As we would expect, there are subcultural differences within these cultural expectations.

Other cultural values also affect childhood. In many cultures, female children were sometimes killed because their economic value to the family was considered minimal. Conversely, male children in those cultures were valued because they could provide labor and income. Similarly, disabled or handicapped offspring were also devalued. While gender, race, and physical ability are viewed today in more positive ways, culture still influences how children are viewed. Cultural norms dictate that male infants wear blue, females pink. Boys are dressed in miniature football jerseys, girls in miniature dresses. Gender-role socialization continues throughout the life course and interacts with social structures such as career availability, subject preferences in school, and role conflicts (being a mother or pursuing a career).

Obstacles. Obstacles for the infant are those factors that impede growth and development. Given the infant's fragility, genetic and environmental obstacles can easily be life-threatening. For the parents, care for the infant can be blocked by a variety of obstacles (non-normative influences).

Biologically, the infant's genetic equipment may be incomplete or partially nonfunctional, a risk that is especially high for infants born prematurely. This makes it more difficult to perform life-sustaining activities or to interact with the environment so that growth and development can occur. This would be the case for infants born without an organ or a limb; or with a defective organ, such as the heart; or with brain damage. An infant who contracted a disease would also be placed at risk. An unusual or undesirable physical appearance can also be an obstacle—for example, a cleft palate, crossed eyes, or a limb deformity. Although these conditions can be surgically corrected in many cases, they may affect the early bonding between the infant and its parents. Parents may also encounter biological obstacles. The blind or deaf parent, for instance, is confronted with different tasks in relating to the child so that its needs are met.

For the child, psychological obstacles are closely related to its biological capacity to perceive and organize the environment and to process information correctly. The development of fearful or rigid personality responses to stimuli can be obstacles to continued growth. These chronic distress responses can also precipitate negative behaviors by others, such as abuse or neglect. Parents' personality patterns can be obstacles when they lead to compulsive behavior in child care that restricts rather than enhances growth.

Social-structural obstacles for the child may include inadequate nurturance, physical care, and nutrition as a result of poverty, dysfunctional family structures, disorganized communities, or adults with poor parenting skills. These factors are also obstacles for parents. Cultural obstacles include beliefs and values that devalue certain types of infants, such as the illegitimate, the "fussy," or children who are members of minority groups. As noted previously, gender stereotyping can be an obstacle for both male and female children when it inhibits them from developing to their full potential.

Cultural systems can also be considered obstacles when they mandate child-care practices that conflict with biological needs. An example is excessively early or rigid toilet training. Another example of cultural values that interfere with successful parenting is when members of certain groups are discouraged from childrearing. In the United States, this applies to single parents, homosexuals, and the physically or mentally impaired, among others. Members of these groups can and do successfully care for infants and children, but they have to fight dominant cultural values and beliefs that view them as incompetent and unworthy.

While the negative effects of prejudice around race, ethnicity, gender, physical and mental ability, and sexual orientation are not fully manifest until later stages of childhood, their roots take hold in the nature of interactions during infancy.

Implications for Intervention. Infants need a great deal of care if they are to thrive and develop. This requires many resources, including knowledge, money, energy, love, food, shelter, and time. Many parents lack some of these resources and have few support systems available to help them. Professionals need to be able to assess the resources available, always taking into account the childrearing strategies appropriate to a person's cultural, social, and physical environments.

The infant may also need intervention. A child born with a genetic limitation or who suffers a severe illness needs careful diagnostic and treatment resources. Parents and others may need financial help to pay for these services, as well as knowledge and emotional support to use them most effectively. An infant requiring special care often imposes substantial strains on the entire family system, while relationships between the infant and the parents can also be affected. The social work practitioner must be prepared to address all of these issues.

The prevailing myth in the United States sees the infant enshrined in a cradle of affluence and acceptance. In reality, babies are sometimes burdens on already strained financial, emotional, or time resources. When they require special care they can be even more disruptive. Understanding the joys as well as the heartaches of infancy as a life stage for infants and parents alike requires careful analysis and sensitivity.

The two-parent family is itself becoming the minority, as is the myth that the mother stays home to raise the children while the father is the income producer. Changes in the family and in the roles of family members require that social structures be rethought and restructured so that they enhance rather than detract from the resources that families need to meet children's needs. This suggests that practitioners must address social-policy issues related to strengthening families and the social structures that affect them, in addition to direct service activities on behalf of families and children.

Middle and Late Childhood as a Life Stage

Tasks. Middle and late childhood is defined here as the period from approximately age 4 to age 12. It is a period during which biological development continues, but comes to be shaped more and more by social interaction in an increasingly wide range of social situations. While basic personality characteristics and gender identification of children are believed to be already established by age 3, they continue to be shaped and modified by their social environment. The child is introverted or extroverted, trustful or distrustful, assertive or passive, but new social contacts and new challenges require emotional adaptability, and they serve to test the child's psychological resources.

The beginning of school is an important task during this period. The child begins a period of significant cognitive development along with the need for emotional control. Gradual movement away from parents and family toward peer groups is normative at this stage. The child has to balance the need for independence of thought and action with the ability to follow instructions, rules, and regulations. There is also exposure to formal and informal values regarding gender, race, physical ability, and sexual orientation. Gender-role socialization is especially pronounced, and exposure to individuals from diverse backgrounds is likely to occur—in a positive way it is hoped.

Resources. To face the tasks of childhood, physical health, personality strength and adaptability, and cognitive capacities form the foundation for incorporating the child into society. Biological resources available to children are similar to those of infants, so they need not be discussed here. Sometimes, though, it is only when a child begins school and interacts with a wider range of people than just family members that particular biological resources are noted. This could include unusually well-developed coordination, muscle strength, hearing, and eyesight, and overall resistance to disease.

Psychological resources also continue to develop from infancy, but they are especially important in childhood. Substantial cognitive development occurs in school and through modeling the behavior of peers, family members, and media personalities. The child whose genetic inheritance includes high intelligence, sound perceptual abilities, and general health has important biological/psychological resources to use in confronting the major tasks of childhood. Physical and social stimulation that confronts children with challenging but manageable stresses helps them develop a sense of competence and well-being. Parental nurturance and support also facilitate the development of a stable self-identity that can adapt to increasingly diversified and new life experiences.

Social-structural resources continue to be important through childhood. Family structure, community structures, school systems, and friendship networks are extremely important sources of opportunities for the child to encounter new people and new situations. When these structures support the child's biological growth and psychological development they become extremely powerful resources. For example, parents who are supportive of exploratory activities by the child and who gently cushion occasional failures help make the world seem a rich and exciting place. Schools that stimulate cognitive and social development by presenting manageable challenges in a structured but supportive context also encourage a sense of security through growth.

Cultural values can be resources when they mandate respect for children's needs and involvement of children in the full range of life activities. For example, in knowing their grandparents, youngsters are exposed to cross-generational learning. Children who participate appropriately in adult activities are better prepared to perform them when they are adults themselves (an example of anticipatory socialization based on predictable normative age-graded events).

Obstacles. Biological obstacles in infancy often become increasingly limiting as the child grows and is exposed to increased demands. The malnourished child may lack the energy to play with friends or to concentrate in school. Limited physical mobility may increasingly isolate a child from his or her active peers.

Sometimes biological obstacles only become apparent in childhood. Hearing or vision impairments are examples of deficits that are sometimes identified for the first time in school.

Biological obstacles become increasingly enmeshed in a web of relationships with social structures, and their ultimate significance in a child's life depends on how these relationships are developed. The child with cerebral palsy who is seen by his or her caretakers as an embarrassment will not receive needed therapy and will gradually become weaker and less mobile. The child with an undetected vision deficit will find school a frustrating and boring experience, and may act out as a result. Even a child who has to wear glasses may be ridiculed by peers and gradually withdraw socially. Mitigating these effects of obstacles requires careful medical diagnoses and supportive interpersonal relationships.

Psychological obstacles are frequently tied to biological and social obstacles. The child with cognitive limitations or perceptual deficits may find demands by others difficult to understand and impossible to fulfill. Excessive expectations or harsh demands may generate fear, anxiety, withdrawal, and rigidity that block a child's ability to utilize existing psychological and biological resources. If the world is seen as cruel, unmanageable, and threatening, then the child's psychological development is likely to be restricted. This will lessen the child's ability to understand and adapt flexibly and productively to situations. The reasons the environment seems so hostile may be biological, social, or cultural, but the impact on psychological functioning is similar. Therefore, we can expect that a child of average intelligence who is regularly pushed into educational and social situations beyond his or her abilities will react with hostility, anxiety, and withdrawal. The amount of interpersonal support the child receives will influence the kind of personality that ultimately develops.

Children may encounter many kinds of social-structural obstacles. Poverty brings with it the risk of chronic ill health, hunger, anxiety over physical safety, and an eroded self-esteem. Racism and other forms of prejudice and discrimination may lead to physical assaults, attacks on one's identity and personal integrity, and social isolation. Dysfunctional families may lead to child abuse or neglect, while unhealthy school structures create a rigid, overly demanding, and non-supportive learning environment. In addition, accidents, natural disasters, and peer groups that scapegoat a child can be significant social-structural obstacles.

Cultural beliefs that lead to gender stereotyping is reinforced in social structures during this time, and they can serve as obstacles to development. Boys play sports while girls become cheerleaders. Such early gender roles reflect later stereotypes of women as supporters of the male breadwinner. Conversely, culture-bound values give rise to negative male stereotyping. Boys are taught not to cry and to see themselves as protectors of girls. These and similar messages tend to cut boys off from their emotions, and they make it difficult for them to relate fully to others as they mature. Other cultural beliefs can also be obstacles, such as those that ignore the child's need for privacy, play, protection, and nurturing.

Implications for Intervention. Opportunities for children to interact with a complex environment are important for growth, but they can easily become overwhelming and restricting. An environment that is too unstructured, un-stimulating, and isolating does not provide the challenges necessary for growth. An environment that is too structured and demanding undermines self-confidence and the willingness to risk, both of which are necessary for ongoing development. Professionals need to assess the ways in which existing environments are able to respond to a child's efforts to understand, adapt, and grow. Sometimes environments need to be enriched; other times they need to be simplified. In all cases, the focus is on helping the child find the resources needed in a particular environment—whether these be family activities, life-sustaining resources, school-system supports, or peer interaction.

Considerable agreement exists among theorists that childhood is a time when the basic personality is established. Although personality is subject to modification throughout life, a view of the world as essentially benign or fearsome seems to be established by the end of childhood. At this life stage, then, the interaction between the individual and the environment is especially critical. Adults frequently have enough knowledge and power to modify the child's environment if they feel the need to do so, but the child has relatively little power to do this. Thus, it is the job of professionals as well as parents to focus on making the environment as supportive as possible for the child's efforts to grow and develop both biologically and socially.

Again, it is important to keep in mind the concept of contextual purity. Parents, too, may be dealing with their own developmental crises. Some of the child-abuse and neglect problems that social workers commonly address may be rooted in the clash between the developmental needs of children and those of their parents. When such problems arise, a variety of social welfare services are available. These include such child-welfare services as residential child-care facilities, foster homes, child health programs, income-maintenance services, recreational programs, and supportive services such as day-care centers. However, practitioners must be ever diligent to spot and eliminate in the child-welfare system those social-structural manifestations of prejudice and discrimination based on race, gender, sexual orientation, and physical or mental abilities.

Adolescence as a Life Stage

Tasks. The major tasks of adolescence, defined here as approximately age 13 to 18, revolve around biological development and further integration into social institutions. Adolescence is characterized by selective biological development, building on the basic motor, perceptual, and cognitive maturation that has already occurred during infancy and childhood. During adolescence there is a substantial increase in physical size, height, and weight. Sexual maturation also takes place, including the emergence of secondary sex characteristics such as breast development, growth of body hair, and so on. The rapid growth in size and sexual maturation is the result of substantial hormonal changes that affect both physical appearance and emotional needs. A large part of the adolescent's task, then, is to adjust to changes in body image, physical capacities, and sexual needs.

These biological changes take place within a social context that is also changing. School demands are more academically rigorous and are increasingly related to lifelong planning. For example, academic success affects whether the teenager goes to college and, in turn, future career opportunities. School also becomes an increasingly important social arena in which peer-group pressure accelerates. Lifelong friendships and interaction patterns can be established at this time.

Biological development, academic demands, and peer pressure naturally interact. Adolescents confront a changing self, making it difficult to understand precisely what their needs and capabilities are. Friendship patterns that characterized childhood may suddenly seem inappropriate as young people struggle to find acceptance among their peers. Intellectual capacity, physical skill, and outward appearance are dimensions that heavily influence the kinds of social demands and opportunities available to the adolescent. This is further affected by the youngster's race, ethnicity, and gender. For example, a young woman who matures and grows in size early in her adolescent years may feel awkward and sexually vulnerable, whereas one who experiences these events later may be more ready to integrate them into her social relationships. The reverse is true for young men, who tend to grow and mature later than women. But the young man whose development is late even for his gender often comes to feel weak and unattractive.

As adolescents move closer to adulthood, their life options are affected by cultural influences based on gender and race, as well as being affected by their own capabilities and preferences. Women are moving into roles that have traditionally been dominated by men, such as doctors, lawyers, politicians, and astronauts. However, the great majority of women continue to be channeled by school and through family and peer pressure into typically "feminine" careers that are often less well paid and less secure than male-dominated areas of employment (Dion, 1984:6–9). Race is also a factor determining length of academic career and employment opportunities, with members of racial minorities having less education and restricted employment options (U.S. Bureau of the Census, 1989). Those with special physical needs can also be deterred by an unresponsive social environment.

The support that adolescents receive has an impact on their development. Parents who experience anxiety over the increasing size, competence, demands, and autonomy of their teenage children may find it difficult to support efforts of adolescents to grow and develop. Anxious parents may try to maintain their control by denying the adolescent's new-found competence or by emphasizing biological changes as a way of increasing the young person's sense of uncertainty and need for parental protection. Other adults, especially teachers, can also reinforce either adolescents' sense of developing strength and well-being or their awkwardness and anxiety.

From society's viewpoint, adolescence is a time of some normative flexibility that accommodates biological changes and sometimes erratic approaches to meeting one's needs. Yet society still expects that by the end of adolescence the developing adult will be ready to assume a relatively stable role in the social structure.

Resources. The adolescent's physical resources are often prodigious. Physical strength and size are powerful resources, as are the continued strengthening of perceptual and cognitive abilities. Adequate nutrition is an important resource during adolescence because physical growth during this time exerts considerable demands on the body. Sexual functioning matures during adolescence and is a powerful motivator for behavior. Psychologically, adolescents learn how to integrate their new physical abilities with social relationships with their peers and with adults. These become important beginnings of support systems that will continue throughout life. Perceptual and cognitive resources are especially important for meeting increasing societal demands for achievement in an expanding range of areas, among which school, work, and family are especially important. Through this process, the personality is gradually enriched by increasing mutuality in relationships, a deepening of interests, and a clearer articulation of personal values and goals.

Social-structural resources are those that promote the adolescent's sense of competence and need for individualization. The family continues to be an important potential source of support, and the peer group assumes increased importance. School becomes a possible source of enrichment, while the developing competence of teens enables them to participate in a wide range of social activities such as driving, working, participating in school- or church-sponsored activities, and so on.

Culturally, values become very important resources for helping adolescents solidify their self-identity and self-image, as well as for helping them order their personal values and lifelong priorities. Decisions about the balance between work and family, self and others, achievement and sharing, and stability and change grow out of cultural values.

Obstacles. Biological development can be an obstacle in a variety of ways during adolescence. The biological changes that occur may not be well understood and may, therefore, create social difficulties. Changes in size and strength can create appearance and behavior characteristics that are denigrated by others—the very tall young woman, or the overly enthusiastic and slightly uncoordinated young man are two instances of adolescents who receive such treatment. Illness and accidents are also possible when physical growth is not supported by adequate nutrition, or when growth between various parts of the body is not synchronous. In addition, hormonal changes are common and can create fairly rapid and extensive fluctuations in energy levels, moods, and sense of well-being.

Physical and psychological changes are closely related because the emerging adult body is a critical component of self-image and treatment by others. The ridicule and isolation that may result from developmental irregularities or problems can have powerful effects on feelings of competence and well-being. This is especially true if childhood experiences have begun the process of accentuating weaknesses rather than strengths. However, perceptual or cognitive capacities can be used to lessen the negative psychological effects of physical obstacles. The very intelligent young woman, for example, may be treated with respect even though she does not conform to prevailing standards of teenage attractiveness.

Social-structural obstacles limit development by restricting access to resources or creating social expectations that inhibit growth. Adolescents from poor families may lack proper nutrition or may need medical care to deal with the nearsightedness (myopia) that often accompanies the rapid growth of adolescence. Families may have unrealistic social or academic expectations for their children, pushing them into situations in which success is practically impossible. Schools sometimes emphasize young people's weaknesses, increasing the likelihood of peer-group difficulties. The peer group itself can be an extremely damaging obstacle if it forces teenagers to conform to stereotyped expectations regarding dress, behavior, and interpersonal relationships.

Cultural values can further exacerbate social-structural obstacles by legitimating disadvantaging expectations. For example, intelligent young women are hurt by cultural values that restrict them to the home, and physically limited young males are denigrated by values that emphasize large physical size and strength. Socialization is a very important part of the adolescent's developing and maturing sense of self. It teaches goals and values that will facilitate the teenager's adjustment to the environment. When this does not happen, the transmission of cultural values through socialization becomes a problem. Such is the case, for example, when gay and lesbian teens are not socialized into productive interpersonal relationships that nurture their own self-image and provide the support they will need to function effectively as adults.

Implications for Intervention. During any type of change, either personal or social, people are put at risk. Their efforts to understand change and to adapt to it need to be strongly supported. Otherwise, the uncertainties accompanying change can gradually erode the person's sense of competence. Supporting people through change entails providing information, emotional resources, and help in keeping the pieces of shifting institutional relationships in balance. For example, social work practitioners often help adolescents to simultaneously manage their emerging sexuality, their desire for rewarding interpersonal bonds, increasing autonomy, and the demands of school. To accomplish this, the practitioner must involve many systems beyond the adolescent and the adolescent's family.

Social workers are also heavily involved with modifying social expectations for adolescents. Although there is some flexibility in role definitions, there are many inconsistencies and strains for teenagers. For example, men are allowed to be more sexually promiscuous than women, so the latter may be punished for behavior that is permitted by the former. Professionals attempt to make social expectations more equitable and to help reduce the severity of punishment when teenagers make mistakes growing out of role confusion and conflicts. This might include helping an adolescent to avoid having a criminal record, being expelled from school, or becoming estranged from the family.

The family can be a significant source of difficulty when its perceptions of, and responses to, the needs of adolescents are inappropriate. This explains in part why social workers so often work with families. Adolescents can appear gawky, resistant, angry, aggressive, and unlovable as they struggle to understand their own bodies, and as they seek to establish themselves in their social environment. It is important to try to help individual adolescents and those with whom they interact—especially family, teachers, and peers—to approach each other with greater awareness, caring, and support. Some social welfare resources to help accomplish this include vocational and educational counseling, alcohol and chemical dependency counseling, recreational services, and family counseling.

The emotional turbulence of adolescence may precipitate a resurgence of unresolved conflicts in parents or caregivers (recall the concept of contextual purity), many of whom are dealing with the transitional crises of midlife. They need to be helped to distinguish between activities that are focused on achieving their own goals, and those that are needed by their adolescent children. As with previous stages, social work professionals must work toward the elimination of social-structural and cultural values that discriminate and inhibit the growth of the teenager's potential. Academic tracking based solely on gender or physical ability should be of concern to the helping professions. Biases, prejudices, and stereotyping lead to inequities in economic opportunities, poor race relations, and oppression based on sexual preference and/or gender that are especially hurtful to teenagers who are trying to become productive adults. On a policy and practice level, such obstacles need to be eliminated. Exhibit 2 at the end of this chapter, which deals with adolescents and AIDS, is an example of a history-graded influence that affects today's cohort of adolescents.

Adulthood as a Life Stage

Tasks. Any attempt at dividing human life into stages is at best arbitrary. Clearly there is much variation in the life tasks that confront adults between the ages of 18 and 75. Indeed, as life expectancy increases (a history-graded influence), what is considered middle age and elderly changes drastically. For the purposes of our discussion, adulthood will be divided into three distinct periods: young adulthood, from roughly 18 to 35; middle adulthood, from approximately 35 to 55; and late adulthood, from 55 to 70.

Adulthood is a time of accomplishment and productivity, probably the period when people are most goal-directed with respect to their own life aspirations. However, society expects that individual aspirations will mesh with societal needs. For example, rearing children requires resources that are earned—and spent—through the economic system. Socialization in childhood and adolescence is the major mechanism through which adults are prepared to work toward their goals in socially acceptable ways. Individual goals and societal goals, then, are assumed to come together during adulthood.

At no other life stage is the individual quite so oriented toward the performance of societal tasks. Members of diverse groups process societal goals and means of achieving them through their own particular values, resources, and obstacles. Rossi (1980), for example, demonstrates that the issues confronting women during the adult years differ considerably from those confronting men. These differences, she points out, reflect not only physiological factors but also cohort variables that determine differential assignment of tasks based on gender. Hanmer and Statham (1989) reinforce this view with their analysis of special responsibility that a woman has to care for others throughout most of her life span—first her children, then her spouse, then elderly parents, and finally her elderly spouse. In a similar way, Devore and Schlesinger (1981) demonstrate how adult development tasks vary among ethnic groups, while Sutkin (1984) looks at physical ability as an important variable throughout the life course.

In addition to working toward the attainment of task goals, adulthood is a time when people seek interpersonal intimacy and when some interpersonal relationships may include sexual activity. Marriage is, of course, one pattern, but others include parenting relationships, non-married coupling, and selected friendships. The adult's twin sense of accomplishment and well-being are, for most people, heavily dependent on the formation of close interpersonal relationships that provide important social, biological, and psychological supports. Although adulthood is a period of autonomous goal-seeking behavior carried out in the major institutions of society, it is also a time of personal nurturance through the special relationships found in adulthood—marriage or other forms of coupling, parenting, and so on. Thus, adulthood is both outwardly and inwardly focused, a time of both independence and interdependence.

Resources. In adulthood, people usually have as many physical resources as they will ever have. Although physical development continues, gradually moving into increasingly degenerative conditions, adulthood is generally characterized by well-developed physical, perceptual, cognitive, and personality resources. Levels of development vary, of course, but they are not usually substantially changed in adulthood. The use of resources can vary, however. Use is a function of social-structural variables that either facilitate or inhibit adult behavior.

Social-structural resources for adults are found primarily in the major institutions of society that serve to organize people's behavior around the performance of significant life tasks. Through the family and family-like structures, adults solidify their most intimate interpersonal relationships. The economic institution is an important arena in which people achieve their task-oriented goals, although women have also traditionally achieved many task goals through their parenting and other care-giving roles in the family. The political institution interacts extensively with the economic institution and also provides opportunities for significant decision making. The educational, religious, and social welfare institutions may also support task-oriented and personal-development goals.

Interactions between adults and social institutions vary for different types of adults. Although the institutional structures support the goal-directed behavior of most adult members of majority groups, we saw in an earlier chapter that members of minority groups may receive less support. Cultural values strengthen adults' efforts to be independent in specified areas of their activities, although this varies for gender groups and for members of different ethnic groups and subcultures.

Obstacles. Illness and accidents (non-normative influences) can occur at any point in one's life, but higher rates of both begin to characterize middle and late adulthood. This reflects the stresses that accompany adult life tasks, as well as the range of behaviors in which adults engage. For example, work-related accidents and illnesses occur primarily in adulthood because it spans the major working years. Also, a great deal of violence occurs in the context of the family, especially between adults. Moreover, degenerative processes related to physical functioning accelerate, most commonly in the areas of vision, hearing, strength, and cognition. These changes are not usually substantial enough to have a major effect on behavior during adulthood, but their influence grows cumulatively.

A major potential obstacle in adulthood is the gradual deterioration of personality adaptiveness. This may result in part from physical changes that are perceived as modifying appearance and behavior in undesirable ways. Even such relatively unimportant biological changes as loss or graying of hair or changes in skin texture can generate anxiety and defensiveness. Adults sometimes deny these physical changes by using cosmetics, wearing different clothes, or even associating with younger and more ''attractive'' people. This can have seriously disruptive consequences for long-established and important supportive relationships with spouses, mates, siblings, close friends, and work associates. Loss of these supports can undermine the individual's personality resources and lead to depression or other types of alienation and isolation.

A second assault on psychological functioning in adulthood results from the interplay of social-structural and personality variables. Adulthood is, as has been noted, the principal period in the life course when cherished life goals are sought through such activities as work, peer relationships, family or family-like relationships. However, it is only in rare instances that all of an individual's life goals are attained, and during adulthood the person has to begin to come to terms with this reality. Social-structural resources naturally play a significant role in an individual's ability to achieve life goals. Poverty, destructive family or family-like relationships, unemployment, accidents or injuries, and the loss of loved ones can all block goal attainment. When these non-normative and disruptive events occur, the individual's own sense of identity, self-worth, and well-being are called into question. Even worse, there seems less and less time left in life to try again. The sense of personal and societal failure is further underscored by cultural values that stress successful goal attainment.

Psychological responses can include a whole range of defensive actions, sometimes even including changing the place in which one lives so that failure will not be so apparent. Cultural values may be especially inhibiting to the efforts of adult members of diverse groups to meet their needs. For example, some homosexuals respond to negative cultural definitions by hiding their true identity through loveless heterosexual marriages and furtive homosexual contacts. Many women accept physical and emotional abuse rather than endure the stigma of divorce—even today when divorce is much more common than in the past. The cost in terms of personal well-being is extremely high for those who attempt to sacrifice one's own needs in order to meet rigid societal expectations.

As the course of development throughout the adult years is examined, it becomes clear that disorder and disruptions commonly occur. Social work practitioners also need to be sensitive to gender, ethnicity, life style, and physical ability as important variables that influence the package of resources and obstacles that help or hinder the resolution of development tasks.

Implications for Intervention. As in previous stages, multiple variables govern the tasks, resources, and obstacles encountered in this long and complex period of the adult years. Both age-graded and non-normative critical life events, as well as history-graded (cohort) influences, affect the need for and appropriateness of intervention strategies.

Adulthood is a time of excitement, challenge, change, and stress. Practitioners should be prepared to support adults and to help them cope with such stresses of adult life as work pressure, relationship problems, and parenting demands. It is also critical that the social structure reward people's plans and activities. Institutionalized discrimination, for instance, systematically blocks the efforts of certain groups to achieve their goals. In offering help, professionals need to recognize that adults are a very special group with which to work. Adults may strongly value their independence and autonomy if cultural values have taught them to do so. Thus they frequently resist offers of help from others, even professionals. A sense of competence is extremely important to adults, and utmost care is needed to support and preserve it. Nevertheless, the stresses and challenges of adulthood often lead to the need for personal support and institutional intervention.

Psychosocial themes that characterize adulthood include companionship versus isolation, and regrouping versus binding or expulsion (Rhodes, 1977). Major changes in family relationships occur as teenagers increasingly meet emotional needs outside the family. Eventually the children are likely to establish their own adult relationships and move out of the family home. Spouses may find their relationship with one another revitalized as they no longer have to set aside their own companionship needs in order to meet the challenge of parenting. Regrouping versus binding or expulsion applies when the children leave the parental home. According to Rhodes, the essential task is allowing for the separation of the children as a natural result of their growth and maturity. The ability to accomplish this task rests heavily on developing a strong marital relationship separate from the parenting function.

Increasingly, however, adults are choosing alternatives to the traditional nuclear family pattern. Remaining single, developing an intimate relationship with a same-sex partner, and having a childless marriage are choices more and more people are making. These emerging patterns bring new life-stage demands for which there are few role models. Practitioners must be aware of these alternative approaches to meeting the tasks of adulthood and know how to help people function effectively in whatever pattern they choose. This may present professional helpers with considerable challenges to their own value system, and they may need to stretch their thinking to learn how these alternatives can be integrated into prevailing institutional structures and cultural beliefs.

Before leaving the topic of adult development, we should note that Gilligan (1982) questions the applicability of a male-dominated life-cycle theory to the experiences of women. Gilligan points out that women bring a different viewpoint, different priorities, and an alternative perspective on maturity. The hallmark of this perspective, according to Gilligan, is a moral understanding based on a greater orientation toward the value of supportive relationships and useful networks of interdependence. For example, women may see strength in interdependence and mutual support, rather than in the more common male tendency to emphasize independence and competition. This view of the world can be a significant resource for adult women, even though their male partners and colleagues may find it difficult to understand. The effective practitioner must understand these kinds of gender differences, providing support where needed and facilitating communication so that greater sharing of gender-specific resources can occur.

Old Age as a Life Stage

Tasks. Just as there is little consensus regarding what one considers adulthood, there is lack of agreement regarding what is considered old age. Some gerontologists talk of two phases of being old, old age and old-old age, the latter referring to the period from age 85 and older—the most rapidly growing segment of our current population. Technological advancement in health care (a history-graded influence), better nutrition, and the somewhat improved economic status of the average elderly person all contribute to the increased life expectancy of the elderly. This may create for many people two phases of aging: the dramatic change in social role that begins occurring at about age 65, and the increased concern with physical changes and health needs that are likely to develop after age 85.

If there is no agreement among gerontologists about what constitutes old age, how are we to understand this stage of the life course? Is it biological phenomenon characterized by physiological decrements? A psychological stage accompanied by sensory and motor changes? A social category defined by an arbitrary chronological age that determines one's eligibility for programs and services? Perhaps nowhere in the life course is the interrelationship of the biological, psychological, social-structural, cultural, and spiritual dimensions of behavior more dramatically observed.

Looking over one's life in order to make sense of it is one of the central tasks of old age. This need not be a time of morbid reflection about what might have been, nor a time spent focusing on one's losses and decrements. Rather, it can be a time of continued psychological growth and development—an invitation to look more deeply into oneself. Bianchi (1986) believes that

> stressing growth through diminishments is not an appeal for a sad and gloomy old age in which one concentrates in an almost morbid way on deterioration and death. Rather, growth through diminishment, based on a willingness to encounter the inner demons of old age with faith, can lead to an authentic joy even among hardships. It is by facing the terrors of old age, by launching out on the final night-sea journey, that a person finds the courage and insight to be profoundly wise for others in adulthood. (p. 188)

Obviously this life stage is one of tremendous change and adjustment, both biologically and socially. Indeed, these two areas interact closely, and the nature of their interaction is the major determinant of whether old age is a time of contentment or desperation. On the other hand, old age may also be a time of freedom from many of the tasks of earlier life stages, such as work. Nevertheless, an increasing number of elderly people continue to maintain active work and professional lives. For them, old age is neither a period of retirement nor disengagement from significant social roles. Whether old age is a time of disengagement from previous social roles and responsibilities, or a time of continued interaction with others, is related more to one's individual style of coping throughout the life course than it is a function of chronological age.

Resources. Although old age entails physical deterioration in a number of areas, most older people continue to have relatively good health and retain most of their perceptual and cognitive capacities until very advanced old age. Age itself, therefore, can be a resource, just as it is a period of continued growth and development. Of course, people age differently, just as they differ in so many other ways, and some people experience advanced physical deterioration at relatively young ages. Nevertheless, most people are able to carry on their usual activities during old age with relatively minor adjustments.

Physical energy is used differently, however, Some older people tend to avoid the hectic pace that younger people prefer and to think through their actions with more care before acting on them. In this sense, the elderly become more efficient, reflecting once again the strong tie between physical and psychological resources throughout the life course. Looking back on a lifetime of accomplishments, most older people find self-validation and satisfaction, and can adjust to lower energy levels by focusing on what is meaningful to them rather than on what society expects. To them, old age is a time of continued social and political activity, and a reference to this life stage as "the golden years," meaning a period of inactivity, might indeed be offensive.

The organization of older people into special-interest pressure groups, such as the Gray Panthers or the American Association of Retired Persons (AARP), has helped strengthen social-structural resources for the elderly. A variety of financial aid programs help maintain income in old age and provide other concrete support services such as housing and transportation subsidies, in-home and congregate meal programs, and medical care services (Ford Foundation, 1989). These services are often needed by elderly people who have limited incomes and who are frail or living alone. Additional social needs are increasingly being recognized and met through self-help groups, the development of recreational programs, the creation of educational opportunities, and the provision of personal counseling services.

There is a special emphasis now on structuring institutional arrangements so that older people can retain control over their own lives. Some programs currently being developed are housing that builds in both autonomy and immediate access to help, transportation systems that are more physically and financially accessible to the elderly, and counseling and financial supports to help link the older person to some type of family or family-like network. Nevertheless, existing social-structural arrangements sometimes impinge on the quality of life of older persons. This is the case when they are dumped by their families in nursing homes, when medical care is impersonal and inadequate, and when their housing does not provide for their physical safety and social needs.

Cultural values have become extremely important determinants affecting the nature of old age, and the self-help groups organized among older persons have had a noticeable impact. When the extended family is a common social-structural form, older people are usually taken care of primarily within the family unit. This is much less common in the nuclear family.

Other values also affect the treatment of the elderly. In a society that emphasizes autonomy and productivity, the elderly may not want to be dependent on other family members. They may prefer to be socially and sexually active even if the primary spouse or mate dies, leading to the formation of new families and family-like units among older persons. They may also wish to define for themselves the extent of their involvement with children, grandchildren, and the economic system, rather than automatically assuming roles expected of them by their adult children. All of these structural changes reflect cultural values that are gradually changing to accommodate a much greater degree of independence and variation in the behavior of the elderly.

Obstacles. Even for the relatively healthy older person, increasing old age brings greater risks of illness, accidents, and physical deterioration. This may progressively limit the person's physical mobility and social participation. It may also strain the financial resources available to the older person. Gradually, the individual becomes more dependent on others. This can threaten a person's sense of self-identity and well-being. Combined with a commonly experienced gradual loss of perceptual acuity—especially sight, hearing, and taste—the older person may withdraw and become increasingly isolated. This often reduces the motivation for living, which can manifest itself in reduced appetite to the point of malnutrition and a lack of mobility and stimulation that then accelerates physical deterioration.

While there has been greatly increased recognition of the needs of the elderly in recent decades, social-structural factors still make this stage problematic. Young people grow up detached from older people and do not learn how to prepare for this life stage. When grown children move out of the home, sometimes called the "empty nest" syndrome, and when a worker has to retire, abrupt loss of social roles leaves people feeling useless and undirected. The high cost of medical care creates anxieties that old age will lead to destitution.

These conditions are perpetuated by cultural values that overemphasize youth and physical appearance, as well as productivity and independence. American society values progress and change and is always pushing toward the new with little respect for its own past or those who created it. In such a milieu, it is little wonder that older people feel left behind and left out. We know only too well that these feelings are closely tied to accelerated biological deterioration, social isolation, and psychological distress. Unfortunately, these are realities for many of the elderly. Many of these realities are reversible, however, and as the aged gain in political and economic power as a result of their increasing numbers and stronger group cohesion, societal resources may be reallocated so as to meet more adequately the needs of those in this life stage.

Ageism is perhaps the major obstacle confronting the elderly in contemporary society. Beliefs about the elderly being unwilling or unable to change, incapable of learning, asexual, rigid, conservative in nature, and dependent and withdrawn are commonly held misconceptions about the elderly. Unfortunately, these negative images are commonly found among helping professionals (Bloom, 1990). If internalized, these stereotypes become the soil for the self-fulfilling prophesy whereby the elderly come to behave in ways that are consistent with social expectations. Ageism therefore is destructive not only to the individual, but also to the social order (Barrow, 1989:10).

Implications for Intervention. As with any type of diversity, old age has its particular resources and obstacles. Society holds conflicting views about the elderly. On one hand, it assumes that older people are physically and emotionally dependent. On the other hand, it tries to find ways to make them more self-sufficient because they constitute a growing percentage of the population. Social work professionals, as part of their commitment to help people live self-directed lives, must reinforce societal efforts to recognize and support the many strengths of older people. For example, there is a need for many more apartment complexes that allow the elderly to live autonomously and still have access to immediate physical help and social companionship. There is also a need for nursing homes in which the older person's right to, and need for, privacy—including the privacy to express oneself sexually—is respected. Many other services are needed as well, especially adequate medical care.

At the interpersonal level, we must be sensitive to the older person's continuing need for friendship, social recognition, and intimate ties to others. An older person may need emotional support to adjust to a radically altered physical appearance or decreased physical mobility. A strong sense of self-respect is as important in retirement as it is at any other point in one's life. Help in meeting daily needs can also be of critical importance. This could include help in such diverse activities as securing transportation to health-care facilities, applying for financial assistance, or filling out medical forms.

Death as a Life Stage

Throughout this chapter we have tried to present a framework usable for analyzing human behavior in its social context at any point in the life course. We have illustrated this framework with the life stages of conception and birth, infancy, childhood, adolescence, adulthood, and old age. Now we would like to give you the opportunity to use the framework yourself to analyze death as a life stage. It is hoped this will increase your mastery of the framework and give you greater confidence in its use. To assist you, we will provide some general guidelines.

Before moving to the analytical framework, it may be helpful to think for a moment about your own attitudes toward death. Most children and young people are shielded from death and do not see it as part of life. Hospitals usually do not allow children to visit patients—they have to be adolescents; children are often not taken to funerals; they frequently have very little contact with the elderly. When something is unfamiliar it often seems strange and even frightening. Many readers may feel this way about death.

Yet today there is a rich literature about death and dying that can help people to better understand this part of the life course. As a professional, you will need to feel comfortable practicing in situations that include death or dying. We have already seen that human life and social structures are characterized by diversity, a fact that professional helpers must learn to understand and appreciate. Both death and dying are components of this diversity. As you use the framework to analyze death as part of the life course, remind yourself that it is as important, as complex, and as fascinating as any other life stage.

Tasks. Think about the life tasks with which the individual and society are faced at death. What does each gain and what does each lose? One way to think this through is to try to imagine what would happen if people lived forever. What problems would be created that death helps solve? Another thought to ponder is why people fear death—what are they really afraid of, and how does understanding their fear help explain the life tasks to be accomplished at death? Does thinking about death in terms of life tasks make it easier or more difficult for you to think about your own death?

Resources. Using the biological/psychological/social-structural/cultural format, determine what resources people have as they try to carry out the life tasks associated with death. Another way to think about this is in terms of those factors that make it easier for people to die. These might be biological factors, such as drugs; psychological factors, such as emotional security; social-structural factors, such as legal procedures to pass on resources to others; and cultural factors, such as beliefs about an afterlife and rituals to help people prepare for death. Resources, then, are the things that support people's efforts to die in such a way as to maximize their sense of personal and social well-being. Does it seem a contradiction to think of well-being at the point of death? Why or why not?

Obstacles. The opposite side of the resource view would be the bio-psycho-social-cultural factors that make it more difficult for people to die. Think about pain, for example. Is it a resource, making it easier to accept death, or an obstacle, making it harder, or is it both? In thinking about obstacles, be sure to include relationships with others. When do relationships make it more difficult to die? When do they make it easier? Do you have difficulty thinking about obstacles, especialy in relation to death? Why is this a painful subject for you? Why isn't it?

Implications for Intervention. To what aspects of dying should professionals be especially sensitive? Remember to think systemically so that you do not overlook help that those associated with the dying person might need, as well as help for the particular dying person. As you think about it, are there resources that professionals might need in order to work effectively in the highly emotional situations in which death often occurs? What might these be, and would they include structural supports as well as personal resources? Could you work with someone in the last life-cycle stage? Think carefully about the problems you would anticipate if such a situation were part of your work responsibilities. How does such thinking help you understand the implications of death as a life stage for the helping professions?

SUMMARY

It is apparent that the life course encompasses a relentless progression of changes. Some come from within the organism itself, and others are created by the external human and physical environment. Yet amid these changes there are some constants. These include lifelong tasks: physical survival, physical development within genetic limits, attempts to relate to others, developing and strengthening a personal sense of self-worth and competence, and task-focused behavior. We have seen how these constants are shaped somewhat differently at each life stage and how there is great variability and diversity throughout the life course based on gender, ethnicity, physical ability, and life style.

Many factors influence the resources and obstacles encountered throughout the life course, and multiple influences (age-graded, history-graded, and non-normative) determine the necessity for, and type of, professional intervention that is needed. Using the life course to understand behavior thus leads back to two important points made much earlier in the book. One is that human behavior involves the interaction between people and their environments. The second is that human beings have common human needs that are elaborated and met in extraordinarily diverse ways. The next and last chapter will further examine some implications of these two points.

KEY TERMS

Age-graded influences. Those aspects of development related to chronological age, and including the accompanying age-specific societal expectations.

Boomerang generation. Young adults who return to their parental home after a period of independent living.

Cohort. A group of people born at approximately the same time and therefore experiencing similar historical events.

Contextual purity. The degree to which one critical life event interferes with other simultaneous events in a person's life.

Critical life events. Occasions in a person's life that signal significant milestones and transition points.

History-graded influences. Societal changes brought about by historical events such as demographic shifts, technological change, and employment rates.

Life course. The period from conception to death that encompasses the totality of the physical, psychological, social-structural, and cultural experiences of life at a given time of history.

Life stage. Any period during the life course that has distinctive developmental and social tasks associated with chronological age and related biological and psychological abilities.

Non-normative influences. Influences on behavior that are unexpected and unanticipated and that show lilttle correlation with chronological age or historical time.

STUDY QUESTIONS

1. Each population of age cohorts experiences similar historical influences as it moves through the life span. What are some of the influences experienced by your age cohort? Discuss how these experiences have shaped your values, aspirations, behaviors, and perceptions of the world.

2. Choose one life stage and one ethnic group, such as a Hispanic, Asian-American, or Native American. For the life stage you have selected, analyze in detail the resources and obstacles the group you have chosen encounters at that stage. After your analysis is complete, summarize your view of the ease with which members of that group are likely to perform the tasks of the life stage selected for study.

3. Discuss some of the resources and obstacles encountered by homosexual men and lesbian women in old age. How do these differ from their heterosexual counterparts?

4. Discuss the properties common to all life events (event timing, duration, sequencing, cohort specificity, contextual purity, and probability of occurrence) as any or all of them relate to critical life experiences in your own life.

5. Read the three Exhibits at the end of the chapter. How has the incidence of AIDS in teenagers impacted on the developmental tasks of adolescence? What history-graded influences account for the changing responsibility of women as caregivers for their elderly parents? Explain the following statement in Exhibit 3: "Girls don't see themselves being what the culture is about. And that has to give them some kind of double vision."

REFERENCES

Baltes, P. (1987). Developmental Psychology. In G. Maddox, ed., *The Encyclopedia of Aging.* New York: Springer-Verlag, pp. 170–176.

Barrow, G. (1989). *Aging, the Individual, and Society*, 4th ed. St. Paul, MN: West Publishing Co.

Berger, R. (1982). *Gay and Gray: The Older Homosexual Man.* Urbana: University of Illinois Press.

Bianchi, E. (1986). *Aging as a Spiritual Journey.* New York: Crossroads Publishing.

Bloom, M. (1990). *Introduction to the Drama of Social Work.* Itasca, IL: F. E. Peacock Publishers.

Brim, O. and C. Rytt (1980). On the Properties of Life Events. In P. B. Baltes and O. Brim, eds., *Life Span Development and Behavior*, Vol. 3. San Diego: Academic Press, pp. 367–388.

Clausen, J. (1986). *The Life Course: A Sociological Perspective.* Englewood Cliffs, NJ: Prentice-Hall.

Covey, H. (1989). Old Age Portrayed by the Ages-of-Life Models from the Middle Ages to the 16th Century. *Gerontologist*, Vol. 29, No. 5 (October), pp. 692–698.

Danish, S., M. Smyer and C. Nowak (1980). Developmental Intervention: Enhancing Life Event Processes. In P. Baltes and O. Brim, eds., *Life Span Development and Behavior*, Vol. 3. San Diego: Academic Press, pp. 339–366.

Devore, W. and E. Schlesinger (1981). *Ethnic-Sensitive Social Work Practice.* St. Louis: C. V. Mosby.

Dion, M. J. (1984). We, The American Women. Washington, DC: Government Printing Office.

Eiseley, L. (1975). *All the Strange Hours: The Excavation of a Life.* New York: Charles Scribner's Sons.

Ford Foundation (1989). *The Common Good: Social Welfare and the American Future.* New York: The Ford Foundation.

Germain, C. (1987). Human Development in Contemporary Environments. *Social Service Review*, Vol. 61, No. 4 (December), pp. 565–580.

Gibson, R. C. (1987). Reconceptualizing Retirement for Black Americans. *Gerontologist*, Vol. 27, No. 6 (December), pp. 691–698.

Gilligan, C. (1982). *In a Different Voice: Psychological Theory and Human Development.* Cambridge, MA: Harvard University Press.

Ginsberg, L. H. (1975). Normative Live Crises: Applied Perspectives. In N. Datan and L. H. Ginsberg, eds., *Life Span Developmental Perspectives: Normative Life Crises.* New York: Academic Press, pp. 11–16.

Gohmann, S. F. and J. E. McClure (1987). Supreme Court Ruling on Pension Plans: The Effect of Retirement Age and Wealth on Single People. *Gerontologist*, Vol. 27, No. 4 (August), pp. 471–477.

Hagestad, G. and B. Neugarten (1985). Aging and the Life Course. In R. Binstock and E. Shanas, eds., *Handbook of Aging and the Social Sciences*, 2nd ed. New York: Van Nostrand Reinhold, pp. 35–61.

Hanmer, J. with D. Statham (1989). *Women and Social Work*. Chicago: Lyceum Books.

Hareven, T. (1982). The Life Course and Aging in Historical Perspective. In T. Hareven and K. J. Adams, eds., *Aging and Life Course Transitions: An Interdisciplinary Perspective*. New York: Guilford Press.

Harper, B. (1990). Blacks and the Health Care Delivery System: Challenge and Prospects. In S. Logan and others, eds., *Social Work Practice with Black Families*. White Plains, NY: Longman, pp. 239–256.

Kimmel, D. (1980). *Adulthood and Aging*, 2nd ed. New York: Wiley.

Lowy, L. (1985). *Social Work with the Aging: The Challenges and Promise of Later Years*, 2nd ed. White Plains, NY: Longman.

Matthews, A. M. and K. H. Brown (1987). Retirement as a Critical Life Event: The Differential Experiences of Men and Women. *Research on Aging*, Vol. 9 (December), pp. 548-571.

Rhodes, S. (1977). A Developmental Approach to the Life Cycle of the Family. *Social Casework*, Vol. 58, No. 5, pp. 301–311.

Rindfuss, F., with C. Swicegood and R. Rosenfeld (1987). Disorders in the Life Course: How Common and Does It Matter? *American Sociological Review*, Vol. 52 (December), pp. 785–801.

Roff, L. and C. Atherton (1989). *Promoting Successful Aging*. Chicago: Nelson-Hall.

Rossi, A. S. (1980). Life-Span Theories and Women's Lives. *Signs: Journal of Women in Culture and Society*, Vol. 6, pp. 4–32.

Sutkin, L. (1984). Introduction. In M. Eisenberg, L. Sutkin, and M. Jansen, eds., *Chronic Illness and Disability throughout the Life Span: Effects on Self and Family*. New York: Springer-Verlag, pp. 1–19.

U.S. Bureau of the Census (1989). Population Profile of the United States: 1989. Washington, DC: Government Printing Office, pp. 36–39.

EXHIBIT 1   WOMEN'S BURDEN IN CARING FOR THE ELDERLY

The following is excerpted from "Aging Parents: Women's Burden Grows," Tamar Lewin. The New York Times, *November 14, 1989. Copyright © 1989 by The New York Times Company. Reprinted by permission.*

Just when they would normally be entering the most productive years of their working lives, more and more women in their 40's and beyond are struggling to cope with the growing burden of caring for elderly parents.

With more people living into their 80's and 90's, these women are finding that the responsibility of caring for a frail parent or parent-in-law can last more than a decade.

While some men provide the primary care to their parents, the usual pattern is that sons offer financial help while daughters or daughters-in-law do the hands-on care.

[A researcher said] "Women can go to work as much as they want, but they still see nurturing as their job. There is a powerful, almost primordial feeling that they have to provide all the care, no matter at what cost to themselves. . . . "

[To provide this care] . . . many . . . [women] switch to part-time jobs, pass up promotions or quit their jobs altogether, finding themselves unable to carry the double burden of career and caring for parents—or the triple burden, for those who must care for children and parents at the same time. And the shift is coming at a time when many more families have come to depend on two incomes. . . .

A 1985 survey by the Travelers Corporation found that about one in five employees over the age of 30 was providing some care to an elderly parent, most often a widowed mother. Most of the employees caring for those relatives were women, even where it was the husband's parent who needed the care. . . .

The American Association of Retired Persons (AARP) estimates that in 1987, seven million American households included people caring for the elderly, and 55 percent of those care givers also had jobs. The association's 1989 survey of working people who cared for the elderly found that 14 percent of the part-time workers had left their full-time jobs because of care-giving responsibilities.

Almost a third of the part-time workers spent more than 20 hours a week helping older relatives with chores like transportation, feeding, dressing, grocery shopping and managing finances. . . .

"One reason older women are so much poorer than older men is that the average women spends 11½ years out of her working life on all forms of care giving, compared to six months for the average man" [said an expert in this field]. . . . "When you quit your job to take care of your mother, you don't get Social Security credits or pension credits."

[For many women] the responsibility comes as a nightmarish surprise that throws their lives out of kilter and makes them feel guilty, inadequate and fiercely resentful of brothers and sisters who are not taking part. One such woman quit her job as a . . . social worker last year after her mother developed Alzheimer's disease. . . .

"I am alternately so sad about my mother's decline that I can't stop crying and so enraged that my life is being messed up that I want to dump her. I used to think I was good at crises, but this just goes on and on, and I'm falling apart". . . .

The number of middle-aged women with elderly parents to care for has increased dramatically in the last few decades. In the early 1970s, only 25 percent of people in their late 50's had a surviving parent, but by 1980, 40 percent did. So did 20 percent of those in their early 60's and 3 percent of those in their 70's.

The need for care becomes particularly acute for the oldest old people, those over 85—a group that has grown from fewer than 300,000 in 1930 to about three million now.

"Caring for an elderly parent has become a normal experience in the life of a family" [said an expert in this field]. . . . "But unlike other life stages, you don't know when it will occur, and you don't expect it to happen. It may be when you still have young children at home or when you are old yourself". . . .

Another demographic trend promises even heavier burdens for the children of aged parents. Because family sizes have been shrinking, there are fewer and fewer potential care givers, making it ever more likely that a woman will end up caring for more than one elderly relative.

[In a recent study] . . . almost half the women caring for their mothers had helped an elderly father before his death and one-third had helped other elderly relatives.

EXHIBIT 2   TEENS AND AIDS

The following is excerpted from "AIDS Is Spreading in Teen-Agers, A New Trend Alarming to Experts," Gina Kolata. The New York Times, *October 8, 1989. Copyright © 1989 by The New York Times Company. Reprinted by permission.*

Alarmed by new data showing that the AIDS virus is rapidly spreading among some groups of teen-agers, experts are calling for an expanded national effort against the epidemic.

Not only are teen-agers becoming infected with the virus, but it is also being transmitted through heterosexual intercourse, and equal numbers of males and females are infected. By contrast, among adults the virus has been transmitted primarily through homosexual sex or intravenous drug use, and the number of infected men far exceeds the number of infected women.

Conditions are ripe for the virus to spread because many teen-agers have multiple sexual partners and very few use condoms. . . .

The number of reported AIDS cases in teen-agers has increased by 40 percent in the last two years. . . .

The Centers for Disease Control in Atlanta estimates that 1 million to 1.5 million of the nation's 230 million people are infected with the AIDS virus, an infection rate of 4.3 to 6.5 per 1,000. And the rate could be much higher in some teen-age groups. . . .

A recent national study of blood samples from hospital patients, conducted by the Centers for Disease Control, found that 1 percent of 15- and 16-year-olds in areas like New York and Miami, where the AIDS virus is prevalent, are already infected. Two to three times as many 21-year-olds as 15-year-olds are infected. . . .

A survey analyzed recently by the New York State Health Department of all births in the state since 1987 found that 1 in 1,000 babies born to 15-year-olds had antibodies to the AIDS virus, indicating that the baby's mother was infected. The study also found that 1 in 100 babies born to 19-year-olds had antibodies to the virus. . . .

Covenant House, which helps run-aways and teen-agers living on the street, found that 7 percent of 1,800 surveyed had HIV infections. The Hetrick-Martin Institute for Lesbian and Gay Youth estimates that 10 to 15 percent of the street teen-agers it counsels have tested positive for the AIDS virus. . . .

Teen-agers are extremely sexually active, as the rates of sexually transmitted diseases among them indicate. The Center for Population Options reports that each year one of six teen-agers contracts a sexually transmitted disease. The group also reports that one of every six sexually active high school girls has had at least four different partners. . . .

[A social worker said] she was chilled recently when she saw a teen-ager infected with the AIDS virus get into a car with a man who had a car seat. She said to herself, "Now that man's going to go home to his wife. . . . "

[Another expert said] that teen-agers are especially prone to deny their risk of HIV infections because they seldom see someone their own age with AIDS. "Adolescents are a prime example of a group that does not look 10 years ahead. . . . "

Experts say that adolescents need a different kind of AIDS education than they are now receiving, one that teaches them to use condoms and that makes them aware that AIDS is a threat to them as well as gay men and intravenous drug users.

When teen-agers are infected, they need to be seen by adolescent medicine specialists attuned to their special emotional and medical needs, not pediatricians or doctors who usually treat adults. . . .

Teen-agers who have become infected with the AIDS virus said that they were not concerned at the time they were infected and gave no thought to safe sex practices until it was too late. . . .

[One teenager] remembers sitting in a high school classroom two years ago and hearing a doctor "talk at us about AIDS." "I was like, 'This is real great but I don't have time for this. I have things to do. I have homework.' I thought I knew everything."

Eight months later he was diagnosed with AIDS.

EXHIBIT 3   GROWING UP FEMALE

The following is taken from "Confident at 11, Confused at 16," Francine Prose. Reprinted by permission of Georges Borchardt, Inc. for the author. Copyright ©️ 1990 by Francine Prose. First published in The New York Times Magazine. *It reports on research by Carol Gilligan contained in her book* Making Connections: The Relational Worlds of Adolescent Girls at Emma Willard School. *The article and the research on which it is based provide provocative insights into issues of sexism in our society and their impact on the development of adolescent women.*

What interviewers kept hearing as they questioned their subjects was that many girls, around the age of 11, go through what Gilligan and her colleagues have come to call a "moment of resistance"—that is, a sharp and particular clarity of vision, an almost perfect confidence in what they know and see, a belief in their integrity and in their highly complex responsibilities toward the world. "Eleven-year-olds are not for sale," says Gilligan.

"I looked at girls at four different age groups, from 7 and 8 years old up to 15 and 16," [says the researcher]. "And the younger girls had a real sense of outspokenness, of claiming their own sense of authority in the world, being very honest about relationships and the things that hurt them." Responding to the sentence completion tests, the younger girls came up with what [a faculty member] calls 'outrageously wonderful statements.' One of them was, 'What gets me in trouble is—chewing gum and not tucking my shirt in,' and then, in parentheses "but it's usually worth it.' "

But as they get older the girls seem to undergo a kind of crisis in response to adolescence and to the strictures and demands of the culture which, in Gilligan's view, sends a particular message to women: "Keep quiet and notice the absence of women and say nothing." Or as [a graduate student] says: "Girls don't see themselves being what the culture is about. And that has to give them some kind of double vision."

"And by 15 or 16," says Gilligan, "that resistance has gone underground. They start saying, 'I don't know. I don't know. I don't know.' They start not knowing what they had known."

This observation may cause many women to feel an almost eerie shiver of recognition, and inspire them to rethink that period in their lives. It will also be interesting to monitor the responses from psychologists and feminist theorists, for [this research] may well oblige traditional psychology to formulate a more accurate theory of female adolescence (an area that's been viturally ignored until now.) Ideally, parents, teachers and therapists who work with girls have begun to find ways to prevent them from "going underground.". . . .

Gilligan's discovery of a crisis in female adolescence is thought-provoking and intriguing, but hardly, it would seem, incendiary—until one realizes how small a spark it takes to kindle a conflagration in the academic psychology establishment. Since the 1982 publication of her first book . . . [her] work has generated heated debate in a field in which it is still thought fairly radical to suggest that women's development might be fundamentally different from men's. . . .

Among the issues that Gilligan raised—and that even her severest critics acknowledge as a valid and important aspect of her work—is that very few of the landmark psychological studies had included women. The models of the "healthy" and desirable life cycle had all been based on the lives of men.

Using data generated by three research studies (one involved 25 Harvard students, another drew its subjects from women considering abortion, and the third involved 144 males and females at nine separate points in the life cycle), [Gilligan's earlier work] posited the existence of two contrapuntal interior moral voices. One of these voices attends to abstract principles such as justice; the other . . . is scored in the more dulcet key of human connection and care—that is, this second voice asks how a moral decision will hurt or help the people involved.

"The occasion for this observation," Gilligan wrote, "was the selection of a sample of women for a study of the relation between judgment and action in a situation of moral conflict and choice." What she discovered was that the ethical distinctions women made were different from those of men: "It was then that I began to notice the recurrent problems in interpreting women's development and to connect these problems to the repeated exclusion of women from the critical theory-building studies of psychological research."

One "recurrent problem" Gilligan identified was that previous studies—based largely on male subjects—interpreted the ability to reason from abstract principles as a sign of having reached the highest plane of moral development. But when women were tested (confronted with classical ethics dilemmas—should a poor man whose wife is dying steal the drugs she needs, etc.)—many of them apparently failed to reach the "higher" level of putting justice first, and so in the language of the profession were classified as "low stage respondents."

What Gilligan suggested was that the second moral voice (which she termed the "care voice" as opposed to the "justice voice") was not fundamentally inferior and less highly evolved, but simply different—more concerned with human relationships than with abstract principles. This corrective was understandably cheering to many female psychologists and graduate students who had been dismayed to find themselves and their sex viewed as morally undeveloped. . . . [Gilligan says] "Care isn't simply a matter of being 'the nice girl' or 'the perfect woman'—it's about being responsible to oneself as well as to others.''. . . .

The source of the change [in the thinking of adolescent girls], in Gilligan's view, is that, during adolescence, girls come up against "the wall of Western culture," and begin to see that their clearsightedness may be dangerous and seditious; in consequence they learn to hide and protect what they know—not only to censor themselves but "to think in ways that differ from what they really think."

Perhaps Gilligan's most radical challenge to traditional developmental psychology is her emphasis on collectivity—in contrast to "individuation," the establishment of an autonomous self that has until now been seen to mark the highest stage of personality development.

CHAPTER 5

Focusing on Practice

Under a government which imprisons any unjustly, the true place for a just man is also in prison.

Henry David Thoreau

Passion, you see, can be destroyed by a doctor. It cannot be created.

Peter Shaffer

CHAPTER OVERVIEW

The purpose of this book is to provide the beginning generalist practitioner with a framework for understanding human behavior. We began with an understanding that as social workers our focus is unique in the helping professions, that is, the person-in-environment view. We have suggested that several screens be applied in the study and processing of the vast amounts of information available to us regarding the sources of human behavior. The text has surveyed selected developmental theories and has given an overview of the life course. When applicable, references have been made to obstacles and resources that either support or detract from positive growth. The text has assumed that the student is familiar from earlier course work with basic psychological theories, developmental theories, systems theory, and economic theories, as well as sociological and anthropological principles. If these theories have not been previously studied it is hoped that this text will aid and encourage the reader to delve further into such material.

This chapter concludes the book by focusing attention on the integration of the previous material into a framework for practice. It also provides guidelines for effective helping based upon a holistic understanding of human behavior.

THE ROLE OF THE PROFESSIONAL HELPER

The profession of social work traces its roots to the late nineteenth and early twentieth centuries. However, the role of "helper" or "healer" within a community has a much deeper and richer history. The role of the **shaman** in various cultures is well documented. The shaman (male or female) was believed to be "called" to the role within the community by the "spirits." Usually this "calling" came early in the person's life in the form of prophetic dreams. These dreams preceded a time in the child's or young adult's life when the individual became seriously ill. During this time the future shaman visited the spirit world and was given knowledge about the sources of both health and illness. Once the youngster recovered and reentered the community, the young person became an apprentice to the tribal shaman to learn the healing arts further.

Having gained knowledge and wisdom from the journey and having completed the apprenticeship, the individual would complete the appropriate rituals and become a shaman. A fascinating autobiographical account of this process can be found in *Black Elk Speaks* (Black Elk, 1979), which records the life story of a Sioux Indian shaman. While the shaman's primary role was in spiritual medicine and ours as social workers has a more temporal focus, we may learn something about the nature of the helping process and role of the professional helper by looking more closely at this process.

The archetype of the *wounded healer*, the person who has some "wounding" encounter (spiritual, physical, emotional) and recovers with increased powers is seen throughout the literature of myth. Akin to the *hero* archetype, the person is called to some quest. The individual separates from the community, undergoes hardships and suffering, gains knowledge and wisdom, and returns home. Exhibit 1 at the end of the chapter tells the story of a nurse named Dusty who served two tours in Vietnam. Her experiences poignantly demonstrate the concept of the wounded healer. Christ, Joan of Arc, and Buddha, are some well-known examples of hero or healer archetypes. John Sanford (1977), a Jungian analyst and Episcopal priest, states:

> The shaman . . . derives his [her] power from a personal, direct encounter with the unconscious inner world; he [she] has his [her] own encounter with the unconscious. The effectiveness of the shaman in helping others stems from the shaman's own depth of experience. (p. 72)

How does this relate to the beginning generalist practitioner? As we have stated throughout this text, human behavior is influenced by many sources. You have decided to become a professional helper. In some manner your life experiences, personal circumstances and choices, as well as many other factors have brought you to this point. You may have particular interests or types of individuals with whom you wish to be of help. You may approach your work with freshness and enthusiasm or you may come with some apprehension or even fear. You may wish to save the world or merely make some small difference.

The choice to help others has its roots in your own personal history. As social workers who hope to assist others in the growth process—whether individuals, groups, or communities—we must first understand ourselves. While physical or mental illness, discrimination, or some other adversity may not have been part of your experience, you have in some way become sensitized to the pain and injustice around you. This sensitivity has "called" you to act in some manner. To begin, however, we may have to follow the path of the shaman and become clear about who we are, what forces shaped us, and where we are going. Such a self-examination is continuous since we are constantly changing.

To comprehend and appreciate our own life course, its sources, direction, and meaning, requires some time for reflection. Indeed, reflection is an essential component in the helping process. To reflect on ourselves as we interact with others, and to reflect on the experiences of others, assists in bringing about the quality known as **empathy**. As stated earlier, the study of human behavior as well as the attempt to understand even one person should be undertaken with great humility.

The anxiety you may feel as a beginning social work practitioner can be minimized if you strive for authenticity in your interactions with others and with yourself. Zen masters speak of "beginner's mind" as being the ideal mental posture. As a novice all things are new and remain open to new information and experiences. Experts, however, already have the "answers" and cut themselves off from new learning. Assisting others depends upon the ability to engage them in some meaningful interaction. To achieve this, certain qualities have proven essential: respect, trust, and empathy. Without these essential traits, authentic interaction is impossible. Beginning practitioners need to be aware of and accept their own strengths and limitations. They should have developed a sense of empathy based upon their own understanding of growth, suffering, healing, and change.

Respect for self and for others is paramount. The health model of practice rests firmly on respect for the individual and belief that people strive toward positive goals. It is helpful to remember that the shaman who misused his or her power was cast out of the community. The role of the shaman was only one of many roles in the community. It carried no superior status. Likewise, social work practitioners should see themselves as a co-worker in the healing process. The healing—whether within the person, the community, or the social institution—

always comes from within. While forces outside may necessitate change, the process of change is always an internal process. We as professional helpers can only assist in that change process.

As social workers, we help in many different ways. In doing so we may assume various roles to assist others achieve their goals: Broker, advocate, activist, educator, lobbyist, researcher, organizer are just a few of these roles. Regardless of the role or situation, the social worker is involved in some interaction with others. While advocating with an income-maintenance worker regarding late benefits for a client, we will be more effective if we understand the frustrations and limitations that the worker may be experiencing as a result of bureaucratic red tape. While attempting to help integrate racially segregated housing, it will be helpful to understand the residents' fears and apprehensions (founded or unfounded) if we wish to bring about fundamental change. Our own values, fears, biases, and attitudes can either assist or detract from our ability to facilitate change in other people and/or in the social institutions in which they live.

As social workers in every stage of our career, we need to take time to reflect on our own experiences and the values and attitudes that we hold. The shaman was usually wise enough to understand which illnesses and individuals would be receptive to help. In a similar vein, reflecting on our own life story will clarify our values and attitudes, which in turn will assist in our work with others. Further, we might ask ourselves some basic questions that could improve our helping efforts.

- What attitudes do we hold toward those we serve or with whom we interact?
- What attitudes do we hold toward certain problems with which we are presented?
- In what way do the attitudes we hold affect our behavior toward the people, groups, or institutions we are serving?

These questions—asked in the context of our basic beliefs about human nature, change, and the quality and meaning of life—provide checks and balances in relation to our interactions with and on behalf of others.

To further the analogy between shamanic healing and social work intervention, we can look further into the beliefs of these ancient healers regarding health, wellness, and healing. Shamans were careful not to overstep their bounds. They were clear that they could not prevent the death of an elder person. It was in fact part of the cycle of nature. They did not believe they could heal all physical wounds. Many illnesses, both emotional and physical, were believed to result from the individual's discontinuity with inner or spiritual forces. The shaman's role was to pray to the spirits on behalf of the person (advocacy), to provide a healing atmosphere for the person, and to assist people to realign themselves with their own natural healing powers.

The similarities to the helping process of the social worker can be easily seen. The social worker provides a trusting, safe, and supportive relationship through which the client can establish goals and the means to achieve them. Like the shamans of old, today's social worker believes in the positive nature of the human spirit. Social workers seek to **empower** the person, community, or institution to achieve positive goals. At times, the social worker is called upon to intervene on behalf of the person in need.

One further function of the shaman will end our analogy. The shaman was called upon to provide some prophetic functions within the community and to guarantee the safety of the community. The shaman was often asked to look into the future to forewarn the community of impending dangers. In this process the shaman provided direction to the community by assessing the wisdom of certain practices. Shamans, for example, were consulted about crop planting, battle plans, and relocation of the community. The shaman's recognized wisdom flowed from the ability to view the situation holistically. Likewise, today's social worker, viewing people, events, and situations holistically, is able to act effectively. Such a vantage point allows the social worker to intervene at many possible points as a helping person. Social workers may work to assist a particular person, community, or institution solve problems (remediation). They may also intervene to prevent problems and maintain health (prevention) by identifying social concerns, advocating for social policy to address problems, and educating people about healthful and supportive life choices.

WHOM AND WHEN DO WE HELP?

Social workers practice in many settings with varying populations who need assistance in multiple ways. The study of human behavior throughout the life course provides some direction in answering the question, Whom do we help? The text has provided you with examples of obstacles and resources to positive human development. A systems approach allows the student to view the person in the context of the intricate networks with which they interact daily. Behavior is shaped by the interactions with these outside networks, which range in size from the family to society at large. Although the specifics regarding the population we hope to serve varies, our task as social workers is generally viewed as assisting the client system to achieve positive goals. Those who need assistance in achieving those goals because access to them is obstructed or nonexistent become one focus for professional intervention. Social workers also focus on the larger aggregate of family, groups, organizations, and communities.

By working to remove blockages to resources we perform *reactively*. When we act to create positive supports for persons, groups, and society as a whole we become *proactive*. A mother of four whose husband has just died needs assistance with burial expenses. She also needs emotional support. As social workers we react by providing emotional support and by helping the woman gain access to financial resources. Women and children are becoming the fastest growing population experiencing poverty. As social workers viewing the single woman raising three children on either a government subsidy or through a minimum-wage job, we see the need to be proactive to effect positive change for these women and their children. An example of a proactive intervention would be advocating for legislative changes regarding an increase in AFDC payments.

A holistic view of human behavior and the sources affecting it not only allows the social worker many possible reactive and proactive intervention points but it demands their use. Such an approach identifies where problems lie and points the way to where effective solutions are to be explored. An example may be helpful. Much concern is currently being expressed regarding the breakdown of the nuclear family and subsequent problems such as juvenile drug use and teen pregnancy. Politicians and evangelists alike lay many social problems at the feet of "failing family life." Moralists suggest a diminishing of traditional values related to marriage and family life as both causes and products of this degeneration. If we define the problems as rooted in moral decay, then it would appear the solutions should be found within the spiritual realm, and religious institutions would become the focus of intervention.

However, if we define the problem as having social and economic origins, the points of intervention would be quite different. As stated earlier in this text, changing economic conditions based upon economic priorities have worked against the maintenance of both the nuclear family and traditional values. Marxists, such as Fred Newman (1988), would suggest that the destabilization of the family is an inevitable result of an economy in which persons are considered to be commodities. In this view, families are unable to cope with the radical and dehumanizing social forces surrounding them.

Social workers can work at multiple levels regarding family destabilization. They may work with troubled children in school, in mental health agencies, and in social service settings, assisting them to "cope" with problems arising from divorce. Adults may seek help from social workers for various emotional and economic problems. However, social workers may also focus on "macro" issues that negatively affect family life and work toward legislative and policy change. Because of their person-in-situation perspective, social workers should utilize both micro and macro approaches to solving problems.

The question of When do we help? can be addressed next. In very general terms, social workers are most often called upon in times of **crisis**. A crisis can be defined as a period when previously adequate resources become inadequate in coping with the existing situation. A crisis state can ocur within a person (job loss), a family (death of a spouse or parent), a community (a natural disaster), a society (an AIDS epidemic), or a culture (genocide). A crisis may be acute or it may be chronic with no short-term resolution (effects of poverty, racism, sexism).

Social work interventions often focus on **transition points**. People approaching retirement after working their entire adult life may easily make the adjustment if they have prepared for that event by making plans concerning the productive use of their time, and by accumulating adequate financial resources. If people are not psychologically prepared, or if financial resources are dramatically reduced upon retirement, they may experience severe stress, hardship, and personal crisis. Social workers can assist such individuals through counseling and by helping them locate social and recreational activities (the micro level). They may also advocate for new policies regarding retirement age, social security benefits, or health insurance coverage (the macro level). These micro and macro interventions seek to reduce the stresses associated with transitions during the life course.

We are, as social workers, also asked to help people change behaviors or to cope with certain difficult situations. The welfare worker who works with children is often expected to stop the abusive behaviors of a parent toward a child. The worker may soon discover that poverty, inadequate education, structural unemployment, inadequate housing and health care are significant stressors leading to the abusive behaviors. As Ann Hartman (1989) points out, situations like this demonstrate the "social control" function of social work. Hartman refers to Bertha Reynolds' suggestion that the social worker needs to be "between the client and the community." Conscientious welfare workers in this situation would, Hartman suggests, " . . . [try] to function in an anomic situation, where there was disjunction between the goals they wished to achieve and the means available to them" (p. 387).

David Wagner (1989) points out that the commitment to social work professionalism and radical change is found to be the strongest at the point of entry into the field and while undergoing professional training. This structural change orientation is gradually attacked by the forces that maintain an unjust society. They push the professional helper to focus on personal adjustment rather than systemic change.

Maintaining a balanced view of the interaction of personal and societal problems is strongly supported by a holistic study of human behavior from a social work perspective. It helps to accomplish two essential practice goals. One, it provides a "clear" vision of where problems and solutions lie. Second, it provides a scientific basis for the poetic truism that "no person is an island." People interact through multiple systems that strongly influence their fate. Empowering people links them with others both for support and strength so that mutual aid and system change are facilitated. Social workers also need to use professional alliances constructively so as to empower themselves and their clients to produce meaningful and fundamental change. When social workers place themselves "between the client and the community" they will always experience the burden of viewing problems as including personal pain and social-structural components.

HOW DO WE HELP?

The most basic tool of social work intervention is the ability to communicate. How, what, to whom, and for what purpose is the grist of the social work process. This section will not attempt to delineate the various social work roles or methods, for these are covered extensively in other social work courses. We will, however, provide an overview to assist the generalist practitioner in analyzing those questions concerning social work intervention.

Current social work practice focuses on **problem solving** as a basic intervention approach. This approach can be applied to the traditional social work methods of casework, group work, and community organization. The generalist practitioner, however, will be presented in the course of practice with many other intervention methods. The choice of method used may vary according to client needs; agency or practice setting values; or mission, constraints, mandates, and personal preference or skills. Nevertheless, it is imperative that social workers assure that their practice methodology is consistent with social work values.

Naomi Brill (1985) provides a schema that outlines the progression from basic values to technique of intervention (Figure 7). In analyzing the schema, start at the bottom and proceed in ascending order to the top. Basic philosophy

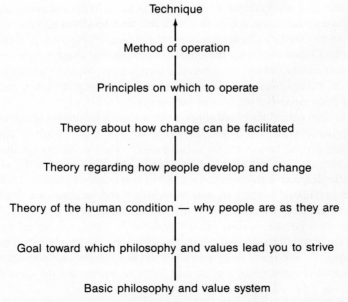

Figure 7. The Evolution of a Practice Technique (*From* Brill, Naomi. [1985]. *Working with People*, Third Edition. White Plains, NY: Longman Publishing Group, p. 180. Reprinted by permission of the publisher.)

and values lead to the determination of basic goals. A belief in the equality of all people would result in a goal of eliminating racial discrimination, for example. An understanding of the negative forces (personal and societal) that trigger discrimination, as well as the positive forces that can be mobilized to eliminate it, will point us further in the right direction. Theories of the change process and methods of encouraging change allow the formation of basic principles, methods, and techniques that can be utilized toward achieving the goal. Legislative and educational approaches are examples of particular methods that could be employed to achieve the ideal of racial equality.

Whitaker and Tracy (1989) refer to five basic social work values that build the framework of practice:

1. Respect for the dignity of the individual.
2. Adherence to a nonjudgmental approach in helping.
3. Respect for the client's right to self-determination.
4. Unconditional acceptance of diversity—racial, cultural, sexual, and political.
5. A passionate and enduring commitment to the poor, to the oppressed, and to the disenfranchised.

These values, in conjunction with the framework outlined in Chapter 1, provide the cornerstone on which social work practice is built. Many occasions arise in practice where methods are not easily reconciled with basic values. Social work practice with involuntary clients (such as in psychiatric hospitals, prisons, and juvenile court) often confronts the conflict between the client's right of self-determination and the various sanctions and methods employed to control behavior. In such settings social workers are often placed in dual and sometimes conflicting roles necessitating ethical judgments.

Professional consultation and support can assist the beginning social worker in these difficult situations. These dilemmas are not easily resolved and can cause distress for the conscientious social worker. They point out the need for systemic changes when social forces have negatively impinged on the client's life course so that few viable choices are left. An example is an indigent person placed in a psychiatric hospital against the person's will because of a display of menacing behaviors in the community. The social worker is faced with the client who wishes to leave the facility and the community's concern for safety. The client and the community present conflicting demands, which the social worker is called upon to negotiate. Such a conflict might be more easily mitigated or even prevented if more community-based halfway houses for the mentally ill were available.

Naomi Brill's schema can also be used in reference to public-policy issues. Social policy and public policy should be based upon and consistent with basic human values. Issues such as health care, minimum wage, housing, AIDS, and family planning are but a few examples of the policies that helping professionals deal with on a daily basis. As such, social work philosophy and values should be essential components in public-policy formulation.

SUMMARY

The systems perspective developed earlier in the text leads us to conclude that the practice of social work must seek to influence all the systems that affect people in need, making both micro and macro intervention appropriate. The human diversity and health perspectives focus our attention on the need to respect the special needs and special strengths of all people, serving them with sensitivity, humility, respect, and skill. However, as important as knowledge and skill are to social work practice, we conclude this book by emphasizing the primacy of social work values in guiding social work practice. In conjunction with an ecological and growth perspective on human behavior, values provide a basis for determining who, when, and how we intervene on behalf of those in need.

KEY TERMS

Crisis. A decisive state in which the usual coping strategies are taxed, necessitating a restructuring of behavioral responses. Crises are often invitations to further growth.

Empathy. The ability to understand the situation of another person from that person's perspective. An essential component of the helping process.

Empower. The process of helping an individual, family, group, organization, or community achieve influence and power in directing either individual or collective lives.

Problem solving. A model of interpersonal helping that emphasizes a systematic, sequential approach to the intervention process based on the scientific method.

Shaman. In many preindustrial societies, a healer called upon by the community to exercise spiritual powers that accelerate growth and change.

Transition points. A change in the direction of the life course brought about by either progression through the developmental stages or by a shift in social status.

STUDY QUESTIONS

1. Working effectively with people requires an ongoing examination of one's motives and beliefs regarding the helping process. How useful is the analogy of the shaman to you in assessing your own motivation for becoming a helping person?

2. Social workers often become enmeshed in the lives of individuals, families, and communities at the time of crisis. Think of such periods in your own life. What forces

or events precipitated the crisis? Was the crisis resolved successfully? What factors helped or hindered its resolution? Consider how professional intervention may or may not have been helpful.

3. Empowerment of individuals and the larger aggregates of families, groups, institutions, and communities often places the social worker at odds with the prevailing belief and attitudinal systems of the culture. What resources might you as a social worker draw upon to strengthen yourself to deal with the problems of racism, sexism, ageism, and homophobia in both yourself and your culture?

4. Figure 7 in this chapter demonstrates how the basic philosophy and values systems of the social worker (largest order of priority) become translated into techniques (lowest order of priority). Think of a hypothetical practice situation and show how the value base of the profession becomes realized through specific techniques of practice.

5. Discuss the implications of the quotes from Henry David Thoreau and Peter Shaffer that introduce this chapter in terms of their implications for social work practice.

6. Discuss Dusty's story in Exhibit 1 in terms of her motivation and choice of methods of helping. Discuss her ability to be empathetic and flexible in her roles with her patients. Discuss her decision about being honest with her patients regarding their condition. How does this relate to your work with individuals, groups, and communities? Discuss the reasons why Dusty may wish to remain anonymous. What does Dusty's story tell you about the nature of the helping process?

REFERENCES

Black Elk (1979). Told Through John G. Neihardt. *Black Elk Speaks*. Lincoln: University of Nebraska Press.

Brill, N. (1985). *Working with People: The Helping Process*, 3rd ed. White Plains, NY: Longman.

Freire, P. (1986). *Pedagogy of the Oppressed*, rev. ed. New York: Continuum Press, p. 28.

Hartman, A. (1989). Still between the Client and the Community. *Social Work*, Vol. 34, No. 5 (September), pp. 387–388.

Newman, F. (1988). The Family in a Time of Social Crisis. In L. Holzman and H. Polk, eds., *History Is the Cure: A Social Therapy*. New York: Practice Press, pp. 126–141.

Sanford, J. A. (1977). *Healing and Wholeness*. New York: Paulist Press.

Shaffer, P. (1974). *Equus*. New York: Avon Books, p. 124.

Thoreau, H. D. (1950). Civil Disobedience. In Brooks Atkinson, ed., *Walden and Other Writings by Henry David Thoreau*. New York: Modern Library, p. 646.

Wagner, D. (1989). Fate of Idealism in Social Work: Alternative Experiences of Professional Careers. *Social Work*, Vol. 34, No. 5 (September), pp. 389–398.

Whitaker, H. and E. Tracy (1989). *Social Treatment*, 2nd ed. New York: Aldine-DeGruyter.

EXHIBIT 1   DUSTY

The following account of a nurse's experiences in Vietnam provides a contemporary example of the "wounded healer." It also illustrates empathetic responses to those being helped and an understanding of the importance of cohorts in understanding human behavior. How did the Vietnam era affect the American populace, and how did historical events help formulate attitudes and values that affected "Dusty" and others during that period? This excerpt is taken from Shrapnel in the Heart *by Laura Palmer. Copyright © 1987 by Laura Palmer. Reprinted by permission of Random House, Inc.*

She went to Vietnam to heal and came home so wounded that to survive she changed her name, her profession, and her past. She agreed to talk about her experience anonymously. "Dusty" was her nickname in Vietnam.

"Vietnam cost me a great deal: a marriage, two babies, the ability to bear healthy children, the ability to practice my life's chosen profession, my physical health, and at times, my emotional stability. After the weight of my postwar trauma reached a critical mass, I changed my name, my profession, my residence, and my past. Silence and isolation allowed me to rebuild a life that for years was outwardly normal."

She is married to a businessman who has no idea that his wife was ever a nurse, in the Army, or in Vietnam.

"When you are sitting there working on someone in the middle of the night and it's a 19-year-old kid who's ten thousand miles from home and you know that he's going to die before dawn—you're sitting there checking his vital signs for him and hanging blood for him and talking to him and holding his hand and looking into his face and touching his face and you see his life just dripping away and you know he wants his mother and you know he wants his father and his family to be there and you're the only one that he's got, I mean his life is just oozing away there—well, it oozes into your soul. There is nothing more intimate than sharing someone's dying with them. . . . When you've got to do that with someone and give that person, at the age of 19, a chance to say the last things they are ever going to get to say, that act of helping someone die is more intimate than sex, it is more intimate than childbirth, and once you have done that you can never be ordinary again."

As a little girl, she adored science, in high school, her guidance counselor suggested that she become a science librarian. She settled on nursing instead, and because she had skipped grades in school, she was a registered nurse and in Vietnam by the time she was twenty-one. She was one of the youngest nurses she knew.

She did two tours in Vietnam, from 1966 to 1968, working in an evacuation hospital as a surgical, intensive-care, or emergency-room nurse. An evac, as these hospitals were called, was the first place the wounded were brought from the field. Once they were stabilized, they were sent on to other military hospitals.

Nurses, it is often said, weren't in combat. It's true they didn't dodge bullets, but they could not avoid the bodies. "The first few times you cut someone's uniform off and the leg falls off, yes, your mind screams, but you stuff that down very, very quickly. You have to. If you lose control, they're going to die. It's as simple as that."

What kept her going then, and what helps a little now, is the knowledge that she was making a difference. She chose to spend a second year in Vietnam because "the wounded kept coming, the war was getting worse, and I was good at what I did." She knew that "these people would have a future because of all of the shit I was going through."

. . . There was an incredible rush that came when someone they hadn't expected to make it through the night went home. Those are the ones she tries to think about. . . .

The horror and the pain come from the memories of the ones who didn't make it. Some never regained consciousness and slipped from delirium into death. Some were angry, knowing they were too young to die. . . .

She never encouraged anyone to deny that he was dying. If a boy said, "I'm not going to make it, am I?" she would usually say, "It doesn't look good." There was a reason for that. She wanted the men to be able to say anything they needed to say before they died.

Intimacy was conveyed in words, silence, and touch. She was never afraid to touch her patients. "Rules don't apply. You're the nurse, the doctor, you're their parents, you're their girlfriend and their wife, you're the only thing they have, and whatever it takes, that's what you give. That's what you're there for. It was just automatic."

. . . David was one of the ones she remembers. Eighteen years later, she wrote a poem about his dying. . . .

There is another boy whose memory was important to her long after he died. She has forgotten his name, but not his face. "He was a little shrimp, probably weighed a hundred and twenty pounds. This kid saved my life. He wasn't even dirty. Not a mark on him. Probably had only been in Vietnam a few days. I don't know what the Army wanted with this kid, a little black kid who definitely should have been thrown back. I picked up his head to turn his head to check his pupils and his brains were running out his ear into my fingers. He had died from a concussive blast. I just looked at that brain tissue and thought, 'Whoever this was, he isn't here anymore. He had a mother who loved him and a future and a past and he came from somewhere. It's just such a . . . waste.' "

It was this memory that came back at a time when she was considering suicide. "I thought about pulling the trigger and splattering my brains all over the wall and I thought about this kid whose brains I had to wash off my hands and then I thought about whoever it might be that would have to come into my apartment and wipe the brains off the wall and wash my brains off their hands and I couldn't do that to someone."

The contributions of men who served in Vietnam were, by and large, scorned or ignored when they returned. But the contributions of women, specifically nurses, were simply unknown. The military, which prided itself on the records it kept in Vietnam—counting the number of enemy weapons captured, for example—cannot to this day say with certainty how many women served. The Army that sent them never bothered to count them. The estimate most frequently given is that a total of 7,500 women served in the military in Vietnam. Of these, 83.5 percent were nurses. . . .

[In 1985] there were two anniversaries: the fortieth anniversary of the end of World War II and the tenth anniversary of the fall of Saigon. She was flooded with images of the two wars that had bracketed her life.

Her mother had survived the Holocaust. Dusty was an only child whose grandparents, aunts, uncles, and cousins died in the camps. It was not until she was thirty-six and joined a group of other children of Holocaust survivors that she began to understand how that experience had shaped her. . . .

"I've tried to deny the past, I've tried to run away from it; that hasn't worked and I don't know what will work. Maybe nothing will. I'm just beginning to find out that I am not alone in the pain and I think that perhaps that will be the way out."

It is surprising, perhaps, to some people, but most who have served in Vietnam, despite the hideous aspects of their experience, do not regret that it happened and would go back. Dusty is no exception.

"I have been privileged to see, in absolutely the worst conditions that could exist, exactly how fine people can really be. To see the feeling these men had for their buddies and the things that they did and the caring they had, I think that's a rare privilege. I think I have been very honored by those circumstances."

Epilogue

The nature of social work practice is by definition performed in a social context. The text has outlined a framework for understanding human behavior in such a context. From that perspective a practice orientation has been established which focuses attention on multiple levels of intervention. As social workers, we confront daily the devastating effects of injustice and oppression. Thus it is essential that in our efforts to eliminate these elements from society we do not employ them ourselves in our struggles. The authors wish to leave the reader with the words of Paulo Freire:

> while both humanization and dehumanization are real alternatives, only the first is man's vocation. This vocation is constantly negated, yet it is affirmed by that very negation. It is thwarted by injustice, exploitation, oppression, and the violence of the oppressors; it is affirmed by the yearning of the oppressed for freedom and justice, and by their struggle to recover their lost humanity.

Index

Page numbers for key terms are in boldface